The Meaning and Purpose of Work

Two seminal crises of the early 21st century – the 9/11 terrorist attacks and COVID-19 pandemic – have led emerging generations of workers to prioritize the meaning and purpose of work. At the same time, other social and environmental crises are threatening, capitalism is evolving, and technology is advancing. In this book, a philosopher and an organizational psychologist who together research meaningful work consider what these forces mean for whether work might give meaning and purpose to our lives or take it away. The authors introduce key concepts – meaning, purpose, and work, among others – and consider how they show up in individuals' experience of work, what role organizations play in cultivating them, and the responsibilities of markets and states to the individuals and organizations working within them. Each chapter includes questions and prompts for review and reflection for students and workers who read the book. The final chapter concludes by introducing an original '6 P' framework for making sense of the functional and moral purpose of work among individuals, organizations, and systems: to pursue and perform, provide and produce, and price and protect work. Readers will emerge with an understanding of the meaning of meaning as well as a practical appreciation for the role of meaning in their own work, the managerial responsibilities they may have for serving the purpose of the organization they work for, and the societal challenges that make the quest for meaningful work a timely imperative.

Christopher Wong Michaelson is a philosopher with 25 years of experience advising business leaders pursuing meaning and providing work with a purpose. He is the Opus Distinguished Professor and Academic Director of the Melrose and The Toro Company Center for Principled Leadership at the University of St. Thomas and on the Business and Society faculty at NYU's Stern School of Business. Christopher lives in Minneapolis with his wife, three kids, and two dogs.

Jennifer Tosti-Kharas is the Camilla Latino Spinelli Endowed Term Chair and Professor of Management at Babson College. She teaches, researches, and coaches others about what it means to craft a meaningful career and appreciate the risks and rewards of work as a calling. Jen lives outside Boston with her husband and two kids.

"This is an important book that everyone should read. Written by two of the world's leading thinkers on meaningful work, *The Meaning and Purpose of Work* is full of real-world examples and personal experiences that bring profound insights from multiple disciplines to life. I came away moved, challenged and inspired to reconsider what makes work meaningful in contemporary society."

– **Katie Bailey**, *Professor of Work and Employment,*
King's Business School

"Finally! A book about work and meaning and purpose that is worth reading. It speaks to the questions that we all have in our hearts. And it gives us a framework for hope. Yes we can create better businesses and a better future for our children."

– **R. Edward Freeman**, *University Professor, The Darden School*
of the University of Virginia

"This book delves into the heart of our contemporary work crisis, exploring how pivotal events and societal shifts have urgently redefined our search for purpose in the workplace. The groundbreaking '6 P' framework, outlined by Michaelson and Tosti-Kharas, offers a visionary approach to harmonizing individuals' needs for meaningful work with society's greater good."

– **Aruna Ranganathan**, *Dong Koo Kim Chancellor's Chair*
in Social Entrepreneurship, University of
California-Berkeley

"The current age of pandemics and disruption threatens our very sense of meaning. In this panoramic look at how work is both restructured and misunderstood in a post-pandemic world, Professors Michaelson and Tosti-Kharas shine a fresh light on the promise of work. Using a colorful array of examples and academic research findings, they offer a striking new framework for connecting task to meaning, and work to purpose."

– **Thomas Donaldson**, *Mark O. Winkelman Professor*
of Legal Studies and Business Ethics, The Wharton
School of the University of Pennsylvania

"*The Meaning and Purpose of Work* shines a lively and insightful beacon on the post-pandemic working world. Full of memorable stories and cutting-edge research, this book is an essential practical guide for those seeking meaningful careers."

– **Jeff Thompson**, *Professor and Director of the Sorensen*
Center for Moral and Ethical Leadership,
Brigham Young University

"This book puts the question of 'what does my work mean?' and 'why is it worth doing?' squarely on our agenda. The time has never been more right for these considerations as we come out of a pandemic life 'hold' with a definite interest in how we spend the third of our lives that we spend at work. And who better to take us through this examination than a PhD in philosophy and an organizational psychologist, both of whom have had consulting and business experience! This book will be an extremely satisfying read for anyone who wonders, 'what's it all about?' It brilliantly interweaves stories of people searching for, finding, and not finding meaning with what we know from the science of work meaning. I felt immediately drawn by the stories they told and then 'well fed' by the interesting science they brought to bear on these important questions."

– **Susan Ashford**, *author of* The Power of Flexing *and Michael and Susan Jandernoa Professor of Management and Organizations, University of Michigan*

"In this remarkable volume Christopher Wong Michaelson and Jennifer Tosti-Kharas offer a deeply insightful exploration that echoes amidst the complexities of our modern world. Far more than a scholarly discourse, this book serves as a compelling call to action for those seeking to imbue their work with purpose and significance. A must-read for anyone striving to find purpose and make a meaningful difference in the world and harness the transformative potential of work."

– **Yohuru Williams**, *co-author of* More Than a Dream: The Radical March on Washington for Jobs and Freedom *and Founding Director of the Racial Justice Initiative, University of St. Thomas*

The Meaning and Purpose of Work

An Interdisciplinary Framework for Considering What Work is For

Christopher Wong Michaelson and
Jennifer Tosti-Kharas

LONDON AND NEW YORK

Designed cover image: "The Sea, the Sky, and the Space in Between," by Beth Slater Winnick

First published 2025
by Routledge
4 Park Square, Milton Park, Abingdon, Oxon OX14 4RN

and by Routledge
605 Third Avenue, New York, NY 10158

Routledge is an imprint of the Taylor & Francis Group, an informa business

© 2025 Christopher Wong Michaelson and Jennifer Tosti-Kharas

The right of Christopher Wong Michaelson and Jennifer Tosti-Kharas to be identified as authors of this work has been asserted in accordance with sections 77 and 78 of the Copyright, Designs and Patents Act 1988.

All rights reserved. No part of this book may be reprinted or reproduced or utilised in any form or by any electronic, mechanical, or other means, now known or hereafter invented, including photocopying and recording, or in any information storage or retrieval system, without permission in writing from the publishers.

Trademark notice: Product or corporate names may be trademarks or registered trademarks, and are used only for identification and explanation without intent to infringe.

British Library Cataloguing-in-Publication Data
A catalogue record for this book is available from the British Library

ISBN: 978-1-032-30934-7 (hbk)
ISBN: 978-1-032-30933-0 (pbk)
ISBN: 978-1-003-30732-7 (ebk)

DOI: 10.4324/9781003307327

Typeset in Sabon
by Apex CoVantage, LLC

To our families and our students

Contents

Acknowledgments

This book emerged from a rare moment of levity during the depths of the pandemic. Wearing a colorful sweater and surrounded by flashing lights, our original editor, Terry Clague, took a break from a Zoom Christmas party with his Routledge colleagues to propose the idea for a manuscript about meaning and purpose. After the world returned to doing business in-person, Terry took a new position, and the plan for the book found its final form with our new editor, Alex McGregor. Over the noise of an impromptu opera performance on the intercom system at the convention center where we were meeting, she gave us the freedom to pilot the book with our students and to finish it with a new timeline and title. We are grateful to Alex, Terry, and all their associates for this opportunity. There are too many academic scholars to thank her by name, but it is not lost on us how fortunate we are that our meaningful work includes studying meaningful work with our colleagues and friends. Still, we want to extend a special thanks to Katie Bailey for introducing us to Terry and for providing feedback on our original proposal and working with us on other projects. Above all, we appreciate our families: Christopher's wife Beth and children Sawyer, Reese, and Esme; and Jen's husband Dave and children Lucy and Theo. They supported us and endured our long hours at work when our plan to write one book turned into two.

1 Does Work Give Life Meaning and Purpose or Does It Taketh Away?

Seeking Meaning and Purpose on the Toilet Paper Factory Floor

The causes of an acute toilet paper shortage early in the COVID-19 pandemic may never fully be flushed out – pun most definitely intended – but there is no scarcity of theories. One demand-side explanation is that remote workers were preparing for an upsurge in home-based bathroom "occasions" while doing their business, so to speak, at home. On the supply side, the inability of the toilet paper industry to forecast the urgency of the situation led to scarcity of this certainly indispensable product. Psychological speculation pointed to a general sense of anxiety, leading some buyers to anal-retentively hoard toilet paper to maintain a sense of control over crisis. Moreover, social media has been blamed for piling on, exaggerating the problem and contributing to panic-buying.

To prevent stockroom shelves from being wiped clean, many retailers imposed quotas on purchases. Stomachs turned when a shopper pulled out a knife in a dispute over toilet paper at a store in Sydney, Australia, while a radio station gave out free three-ply prizes to lucky listeners. In Hong Kong, police sniffed out a scheme among armed robbers who stole hundreds of rolls from a delivery truck. While price gougers hawked hand sanitizer for $ US 60 a bottle, tissue was going for the bloated price of $ US 10 per roll.

This was the closest toilet paper would come to being a luxury good since it replaced the reusable sponge, the washcloth, or – eww – the common shirt sleeve. But it is hardly a smear on the industry's reputation to admit that making the stuff remained an unglamorous occupation. The production process for toilet paper begins with digesting trees into a pulp, which then goes through a long and circuitous tract that cleans, presses, and packs sheets of soft tissue into massive – er – logs, which are then cut into the familiar figure of the standard toilet paper roll.

In order to address demand squeeze for their coveted product, toilet paper manufacturers kept factory floors open and got the bowels of dormant production facilities moving again. Meanwhile, executive offices shuttered indefinitely, confirming that "bullshit jobs," to quote David Graeber – as opposed to the "shit jobs" of making TP – could go down the drain without anyone

DOI: 10.4324/9781003307327-1

noticing. A manufacturing facility in Mehoopany, Pennsylvania, stayed open 24 hours to maximize throughput while minimizing workers' exposure to the virus, staggering shifts and distancing employee workstations to prevent spread along the assembly line. Even Procter & Gamble office workers were called to do shifts on the Charmin factory floor to maintain the regularity of production schedules.

As with other frontline, essential workers during the pandemic who showed up to provide healthcare, transportation, and other necessary goods and services that consumers and citizens may not have realized they could not do without, the conditions created by the pandemic, at least for a time, conferred meaning and purpose on the crappy work of the toilet paper factory floor. According to the president of the Consumer Brands Association, a trade organization for manufacturers of grocery products, "[Making toilet paper has] created a degree of pride. It's created a degree of passion."

In full seriousness, to borrow phrasing from Thomas Hardy's tragic *The Mayor of Casterbridge*, the toilet paper story provided but an occasional episode of levity in a general drama of pain produced by COVID-19. As of this writing, more than three years after the World Health Organization declared a pandemic on March 11, 2020, nearly 7 million people have died from the disease, including more than 1 million Americans. The Organisation for Economic Cooperation and Development estimated, a year after the onset of the pandemic, that around 22 million people in affluent countries had lost their jobs and 21 million more remained at risk if temporary job-retention schemes eroded.

Death and loss throughout history have led human beings to wonder about the meaning and purpose of life, and the pandemic was no different. In this book, we will consider the meaning and purpose of work as a central domain of human activity that perhaps makes life worth living at the same time that it has the potential to stand in the way of the good life.

Seeking Meaning and Purpose After 9/11

Our scholarly partnership was borne of our motivation to make sense of another tragedy – the 9/11 terrorist attacks, which claimed 2,977 innocent lives in 2001. At the time, we were both living in New York City where, a few miles south of the main offices of the large management consulting firms that employed us, most of those lives were lost when terrorists used airplanes to destroy the Twin Towers of the World Trade Center. When the attacks occurred, Christopher was on his way to a client's office in Washington, within sight of the Pentagon – another terrorist target – and Jen was waking up in her Upper East Side apartment after pulling an all-nighter for work. The attacks led us to reconsider the meaning and purpose of our work. A year later, Christopher – who had earned his Ph.D. in Philosophy from the University of Minnesota before he went into consulting aspiring to help businesses make the world a better place – had become a full-time visiting lecturer at the Wharton School of the University of Pennsylvania while remaining a part-time management consultant with the same firm in New York City. At the same time, Jen – who had earned her bachelor's degree from Wharton before she went into strategy consulting – was applying to graduate school at New York University's Stern School of Business, where she would go on to get her Ph.D. in organizational behavior. Not long after Christopher left Wharton for NYU, we were introduced by Amy Wrzesniewski – Jen's doctoral advisor and a prominent social scientist studying the different orientations people have that help to determine the meaning of their work in their lives.

Questions of meaning and purpose are central to both of our disciplines – philosophy and psychology. The foundational question of philosophical ethics is, "How should one live?" This sentiment is expressed in Socrates' famous claim in Plato's *Apology* that "the unexamined life is not worth living" – incited by his observation that many of his contemporaries accepted reality at face value and failed to dig deeper and challenge convention. In *The Ethics of Ambiguity*, the modern existentialist philosopher Simone de Beauvoir questioned her contemporaries who doubted whether life has meaning and purpose, contending that people are free to choose lives of meaning, and that nihilism misuses that freedom.

Whereas philosophers study meaning and purpose *prescriptively* – how we *ought* to live – psychologists often study them *descriptively* – how we *do* live in reality. Nonetheless, philosophers and psychologists come to some similar, or at least complementary, conclusions. In *Man's Search for Meaning*, Viktor Frankl, a psychiatrist and Holocaust survivor, claimed that meaning is a central motivational force in human life that can be pursued even in the depths of despair in a concentration camp. Terror Management Theory suggests that human beings look to join communities to be part of something bigger than themselves and sometimes appeal to spiritual quests to stave off oblivion and meaninglessness.

A few years after we became colleagues and friends, we (Christopher and Jen) were talking about our respective experiences on 9/11 and our shared experience of reading the *New York Times*' "Portraits of Grief." The Portraits were short sketches based on conversations with close relations written by journalists about most of the 9/11 victims that appeared in serial form in the newspaper in the weeks following the attacks. The Portraits accounted not only for why victims were at an attack site – most often because of their work – but also sought to depict what made each of their lives unique and meaningful. Some of them focused on work as a central source of meaning – such as the camaraderie and competition among financiers sitting shoulder-to-shoulder, trading bonds and playing practical jokes on each other – and purpose – including the solemn promise among first responders to risk their own lives to save those of others. Many portraits, however, treated work as incidental to or even as a distraction from a meaningful life, suggesting that the victim's work was at best a means to the end of what made life worth living – family, friends, non-work avocations, or even the possibility of a future career to which they aspired.

We spent much of the next few years studying the Portraits to examine, psychologically, how work, in the eyes of close relations, might have given meaning and purpose to victims' lives – or sometimes might have taken it away in the form of unfulfilling work, "counting the days to retirement" or living in "commuter hell." At the same time, the Portraits contained philosophical insights into how close relations wished for victims' lives to be, representing ideals about heroism and home life and reflecting social values as more conventional obituaries often do, according to journalism scholar Janice Hume. Our 9/11 research on the place and priority of work worth doing in a life worth living became the basis of several scholarly papers that inform this book and was the impetus for our first book together, *Is Your Work Worth It? How to Think About Meaningful Work*.

Seeking Meaning and Purpose in the COVID-19 Pandemic

Naïvely, we thought that 9/11 would be the defining tragedy of our work and lives but as we worked on our 9/11 research through the pandemic, we came to realize that, much as 9/11 led many people to reconsider the meaning and purpose of their work, the pandemic did so too. As with 9/11, the pandemic demanded risk-taking and heroism on the part of some workers, especially healthcare professionals and other frontline essential workers who put themselves in peril so that others could live. Similar to 9/11, the pandemic cut too many lives short, including those of many people experiencing the everyday struggle of putting in their time at work while still leaving time for life outside of work – not knowing that their days were numbered. Perhaps unlike 9/11, the pandemic not only influenced the reasons *why* we work but also changed *how* we work – both in the way technology augmented or replaced some human work or enabled other human work that was previously performed in a workplace during "working hours" to be done from anywhere, at any time.

The overall effects of the pandemic on work are complicated and vary significantly by industry, gender, and social location, among other factors. In the United States, the sectors that were hit hard and early were generally those employing low-wage workers, especially persons of color working in hospitality and leisure in urban locations. Internationally, women were more likely to be employed in the service sectors and informal economies and to shoulder a disproportionate amount of unpaid work at home, exacerbating the gender gap in employment and pay.

A sense of "existential terror" prevailed among workers struggling to survive economically, especially within industries in which workers had no choice but to show up and risk exposure to the virus. Designated "essential workers" or "key workers," people in these occupations were determined to be indispensable to the availability of basic products and services. It might have been a blessing for job security, but it was also a curse for job safety.

Healthcare workers were faced with the impossible choice between serving patients gasping for air and ensuring their own survival, enduring through wave after wave of infection. Nightly applause in cities for care providers on the frontlines sometimes gave way to emotional and physical exhaustion. On meatpacking factory floors in the United States, a nation's carnivorous appetite came at the expense of a virus spreading dangerously among mostly immigrant laborers in closely-spaced workstations performing the gruesome operation of disassembling, processing, or euthanizing.

Many workers in the COVID economy belonged to one of three categories: unemployed or underemployed, including mostly women who left their jobs to care for children suddenly schooling from home; frontline workers who often risked the most to be paid the least; and privileged professionals who worked remotely from the safety of their homes with office attire on top and pajamas on the bottom, out of view of their Zoom cameras. While the reality is much more complicated than that, a substantial enough portion of the workforce not only learned to work remotely but preferred it to the passé daily commute, leading overall job satisfaction to reach an all-time high in the United States in 2023.

While technology made remote work possible for office workers, technology claimed the jobs of some service workers as online commerce proliferated, "contactless" self-service kiosks appeared, and warehouses were increasingly staffed by robots. All of these changes led trend analysts to forecast the future of work while workers contemplated their own futures. Some worried that technological unemployment had finally arrived, almost a century after John Maynard Keynes originated that term as a future to look forward to that would enable lives of leisure. Others anticipated that workers would have to be more adaptable to occupational mobility and transitions as technology changed their jobs or rendered them redundant.

Somewhere between the pandemic's real job losses and this hypothetically jobless future, workers in droves commenced a voluntary exodus from workplaces. This so-called Great Resignation was driven by a variety of motivations, including a search for work that was less exhausting, more fulfilling, better paying, more respected, permanently remote, among other preferences. Other quippy terms were coined via social media to describe related phenomena such as "quiet quitting" – showing up for work to collect a paycheck but not going above what is specified in the job description – and "lazy girl jobs" – intentionally finding work that paid well enough to enable one's lifestyle while not demanding significant effort at – or, most importantly, outside of – work.

These phenomena led workers during and since the pandemic to wonder about the meaning and purpose of work, much as they had after 9/11. When the *New York Times* developed a series of more than 500 profiles of famous, infamous, and ordinary people who succumbed to COVID-19 called "Those We've Lost," modeled on the "Portraits of Grief," we embarked upon another study similar to our 9/11 study. While both sets of research arise from unthinkable tragedies, we sought to study them for positive reasons – to honor lives lost by learning from them to guide the lives and work of those, like all of us, who survived. In technical terms, we studied these memorials both for their descriptive insight into human life and work but also to point us toward prescriptive ideals about how human beings ought to live and work.

Of course, all stories of 9/11 and pandemic victims are touched by tragedy, but they are also full of humor, inspiration, meaning, and purpose. They provided the timely impetus for our research on the meaning and purpose of work, and we will draw on them throughout this book. However, they only made the topic more urgent in our minds because they and other stories from our experience, history, and literature remind us of the timelessness of the human quest for meaning and purpose of which the purported urgency of work too often gets in the way. Whether you are reading this book with the pandemic as part of your recent story or as past history, its impact on how people worked at the time is also an opportunity to consider why you work – or have worked in the past or will work in the future – and what and whom that work is for.

Work as a Source of Meaning and Purpose: Market Fit, Service to Others, Self-Realization

If the goal of studying the meaning of life is to understand what makes life worth living, we study the meaning of work to consider what makes work worth doing. However, as the title of this chapter suggests, work has the potential to contribute meaning and purpose to our lives, but it also has the potential to detract from our lives. Unraveling the meaning of work in our lives can be complicated because – as we have already seen with the toilet paper example – the same work can mean different things to different people at different times. Most of the time, toilet paper and other essential goods and services that we require for our hygiene and health are taken for granted. However, in times of crisis, it can be satisfying when other people stand up and take notice of the way in which this work makes a critical contribution to their lives.

But what about in the ordinary course of our work – and not just during extraordinary times? We are seeking to answer the question of what work has the potential to confer meaning and purpose for all people all the time, not just for some people some of the time – and what kinds of work take meaning and purpose away. To search for an answer, we looked for universal themes contained within particular stories of "Those We've Lost." As with our 9/11 research, studying the stories of completed lives – though far from complete stories at a few hundred words on average – was a way of understanding how work was perceived by close relations to fit into the context of the life stories of these people. Some of the subjects of these stories died heroically because the essential work they performed during the pandemic exposed them to the virus, whereas others probably contracted the virus for reasons unrelated to their work. Aside of course from their cause of death, many of the stories of their lives had little to do with the pandemic, tracing their subjects' work that began and sometimes even ended well before the pandemic became reality. With regard to our question, we did not find that one or the other is always true – that work always adds to or detracts from life. Rather, we found a multiplicity of ways in which work can give life meaning and purpose – and a multiplicity of ways in which it can take it away.

Work and Market Fit: Who We Are, What We Do, How We Live

Perhaps, however, it takes a pandemic or other catastrophe to lead us to ask the question. Typically, we work for material sustenance without giving thought to meaning and purpose. Sociologist Russell Muirhead refers to this as working for *market fit* – when the market will pay us for the skills and services that are a good fit with what the market demands. For example, in search of market fit, James Bidgood moved from a small, midwestern town to the big city where he might make it big as an entertainer. Margaret Rossi was a gift shop owner who moved her store next door when she and her husband could no longer pay the rent. And, Aruká Juma was the last surviving member of the Juma tribe for which he was named, who hunted and gathered from the land where he was raised. Though these people's stories end the same way – succumbing to the COVID-19 virus – what we can learn from each of them is distinct. On the face of it, these three stories depict how the work we do is a response to both market and material forces beyond our control. In the arts and entertainment, we go in search of an audience; when the costs of doing business rise, we move or close our doors; and when we are hungry, we take what the land has to give. However, within the details of each of these stories, we can discover not only the willpower, creativity, and determination of their subjects but also a treasure trove of meaning and purpose.

James Bidgood's name may not be well known to commercial moviegoers, but he "was the anonymous director behind *Pink Narcissus*, a gay film released in 1971 that became something of a cult classic" – and one that some observers at the time incorrectly guessed had been made by Andy Warhol. Mr. Bidgood was also renowned among photographers for bringing the style of pornographic photography that made women look like "beautiful angels" to gay men's photography that expressed "lavish fantasies full of references to mythology, adventurous lighting and props, and attractive men."

It may seem strange that the first individual work story we are sharing in a book about the meaning and purpose of work is that of a porn photographer, and it raises an important question: Are meaning and purpose in the eye of the beholder – in this case, the person holding the job – or are they objectively determined, in the sense that some occupations – perhaps including porn photography – are less meaningful because they are not seen to serve essential societal purposes? Who gets to decide? We will encounter those questions again later, but suffice it to say for now that we think there may be good reasons to acknowledge the meaning and purpose that work may have conferred on James Bidgood's life. For one thing, he was a gay man who came of age in an era during which gay men could not see themselves in the fantasies that were displayed for straight men's entertainment. In the words of one critic, he was "a brave pioneer at a time when art photography was overwhelmingly straight." Although we recognize that using anyone's body for others' pleasure risks exploitation, we also are receptive to the possibility that objectifying the human figure can be crude much of the time, though it can be art some of the time. Bidgood's body of work showed how finding a fitting market for the work we do also has the potential to express *who we are.*

It may be self-evident that work is also *what we do* for a living, but can the invisible hand of the marketplace confer meaning and purpose as though it were the hand of God? A rational economic conception of market fit suggests that we ought to respond to market demand by supplying what we can produce at the greatest comparative advantage. While this may be how the market functions from a distance, at close range, *what we do* often reveals the visible hand of our preferences that reflect *who we are.* For example, the inventory of Margaret Rossi's gift shop consisted of "figurines of saints, records of Neapolitan songs, mandolin sheet music, pasta cutters, espresso machines, and little red horn amulets that are used for protection against the evil eye" that kept the culture of her historic Little Italy locale going as gentrification shrank the neighborhood around her store. When the pandemic arrived and tourism shut down, it may have made more financial sense to close the business, but instead, she and her husband "burned through their savings to keep it going." Ms. Rossi's story suggests that, if we were compelled to stop working, we would lose a source of meaning and purpose that motivates us to go on doing what we do. While Margaret was sick with COVID-19, her husband Ernest told her that they could close the business, but she insisted that they would "make it work." Her story shows that, if meaning and purpose can emerge from the abstract machinations of the marketplace, it might be in the form of finding real alignment between what the market needs and wants and what we are uniquely fit to supply.

The story of Aruká Juma shows how work can be inseparable from *how we live.* When he was born a member of the Juma tribe in the Amazon rainforest, scarcely more than 100 of them remained, "ravaged over years by disease and successive massacres by rubber tappers, loggers, and miners." Their way of life was incompatible with that of market speculators. The tribe dwindled to six after another massacre in 1964, and "in 1999, with the death of his brother-in-law, [Aruká] became the last remaining Juma male. The tribe's extinction was assured." Mr. Juma's work was to subsist off the land – "he hunted, fished and farmed manioc, fruits and nuts." Over the years, doing so became more difficult as, "under murky circumstances, federal officials removed him and his family from their land" under the pretense that they would merge with another tribe to preserve their culture. His daughters married into the other tribe, but Mr. Juma's work became to advocate for a return to his ancestral home, where he lived for most of his final decade. But it was perhaps too little, too late. Some features of how the Juma tribe lived were "forever lost" with the passing of "the last fluent speaker of the tribe's language" and the last practitioner of "many of his people's traditions and rituals." Are living off the land and performing rituals work, and by extension, does "market fit" refer to societal fit in this case? Sociologist of work Paul Ransome says that our modern understanding of work as something we do for pay is influenced substantially by what the government classifies as work for purposes of taxation. Whether the meaning of "work" must be tied to pay is another question that will recur in this book, but here, we will remark that Mr. Juma's efforts to hunt and gather were probably more physically arduous than tax accounting, management consulting, and many other activities that society uncontroversially considers to be "hard work."

Work and Service to Others: A Higher Purpose, Caring for Others, Supporting Family

When we think of meaning and purpose in and at work, we stereotypically are engaged in what philosopher Joanne Ciulla refers to as "the search for something more." Working for money or market fit may feel necessary, but it does not always feel noble. Market fit aside, philosopher Norman Care posits that we have two reasons to aspire toward a career: to improve the state of the world for everyone – what he referred to as *service to others* – or to look out for our personal well-being – referred to as *self-realization*. Taking stock of the state of the world and its problems when he was writing in 1984, Care observed many of the same problems that persist in our world today: war, poverty, environmental degradation, and so on. He concluded that, if we must decide between service to others and self-realization, in a world in need we are obligated to choose service to others.

It may be obvious that saving others' lives provides a purpose worth working for. However, Dennis Smith's account of his work as a firefighter gave voice to both the depths of despair that firefighters experience and the heights of heroism that they demonstrate. Mr. Smith was not a stereotypical firefighter, falling into the profession after enlisting in the Air Force as an alternative life path suggested by a "sympathetic judge" when he "was headed for jail as a juvenile delinquent." He rose to become the founding chairman of the New York City Fire Museum as well as the founder of *Firehouse* magazine, an outlet for his exceptional literary talent that led him to publish 16 books. Of the despair in his work, he wrote, "I have watched friends die, and I have carried death in my hands. With good reason have Christians chosen fire as the metaphor of hell." And of the heroism, he recalled the tear-filled reaction of a colleague to the death of a baby, writing, "I wish now that each man who intends to file for the coming fireman's test could have seen the humanity, the sympathy, and the sadness of those eyes, for they explained why we fight fires."

Whereas the firefighter may be the archetypal hero who risks personal peril for the safety of others, the home health aide may be the most under-appreciated exemplar of service to others and unselfishness at work. Both professions exemplify the way in which *caring for others* gives work meaning and purpose. As a case in point, Bibi Romeiza John "was a caregiver for her entire life," which took her from Guyana to the United States "where she took particular pride in caring for older people." As the title suggests, home health aides work within patients' homes, sometimes staying there overnight when a sick person requires constant care and even becoming an honorary part of the family, as in the case of a dementia patient whose family recon-ciled with her help at his deathbed. Of her work, her husband said after she died, "caring for people came so naturally to her that she never considered it work. It was more like a labor of love."

In the course of earning her living, Ms. John bought her family a home and hoped someday to own her own home healthcare agency. In that sense of her story and in that of Suk-joong Song, work not only can involve car-ing for others but also *supporting family.* Mr. Song's story of social mobility began in Seoul, South Korea, where he was a successful businessman in a period of social unrest. He upended his career out of concern for his chil-dren, immigrating to the United States where he would open a dry-cleaning business that "became a neighborhood institution." When unrest came to his American home during the riots following the verdict of the Rodney King case, customers and other members of the community stood guard in front of the store to protect it. Although doing others' laundry was humble and hard work, his daughter recalled the reasons he did it, concluding that when it comes to caring for one's family, "He didn't even see it as a sacrifice."

Work and Self-Realization: Fulfilling Potential, Togetherness, All of the Above

Although Care prioritizes service to others over self-realization, he concedes that the very best form of work is that which serves both ends at the same time. For example, Helen Etuk was a college student who was raised in a single-parent household and aspired to become a pediatrician who would provide care to children, even if their parents could not afford to pay. She regretted returning to school where she suspects she caught the virus, but the reason she was so intent upon attending class was to advance her quest to *fulfill her potential.* Her mother lamented that "She would have done so much," had she survived, demonstrating that doing work with meaning and purpose sometimes involves a lifelong pursuit that begins even before our formal entrance into the workforce.

In the case of Rosendo and Rogelio Mendoza, what gave work mean-ing and purpose was a continuation of their lifetime of shared aims and *togetherness.* Twin brothers and manual laborers whose last job was to weld metal to build anchors for oil rigs, they had dropped out of high school years before to help on the family farm. Their story suggests that their passion was not the work itself, but rather their camaraderie with each other. Their mother recalled that, when they were adults, when one of them found a job, they would ask the employer to hire their brother at the same time. They lived, worked, and died together, born minutes apart and dying of COVID on the same day.

We have centered each of these stories on one particular theme or way in which work has the potential to add to life's meaning and purpose, but the story of Christine Nofchissey McHorse demonstrates the reality that most stories transcend these themes. The same work that achieves market fit can also provide service to others and be a source of self-realization. According to Ms. McHorse's husband, early in her career as a ceramicist, she sold pottery at the Santa Fe Indian Market, carrying pieces "while they were still warm to sell, to pay the electric bill." Eventually, her work came to be recognized by collectors and museums, serving others by advancing societal awareness of Native American arts. However, Ms. McHorse had not yet realized her full potential as an artist. Later in her career, she began combining artistic traditions and developing abstract sculptures and moving "away from the artisanal toward fine art" and to a "sense of freedom in creating her singular work."

The previously mentioned stories show that the human experience of work can be full of meaning and purpose. At the same time, they suggest that the experience of meaning and purpose may vary based on the sort of work we do, who we do it for, and who is doing it. In other words, meaning and purpose of work may be influenced by the context of the world around work, in the well-being of its beneficiaries, or in the worker. When they are in the world, they might exist in the market fit between what the world demands and what we have to offer it. When they are in the well-being of beneficiaries, they can be found in those whose needs and wants are served by the work. When they are in the worker, perhaps they are discovered in the intrinsic satisfaction we experience as creators of work that is worthwhile.

Work as an Impediment to Meaning and Purpose

The foregoing stories from "Those We've Lost" show how we can make sense of the triumphs and even the struggles of work when we consider it in the context of complete lives. However, notwithstanding these myriad ways in which the work we do can supply market demands, serve others, and cultivate self-realization, the more familiar narrative of work in the modern world is one in which work is more likely to take meaning and purpose away from our lives than to add to them. If work can constitute market fit, it can also remind us of the ways in which the things we wish to spend our time doing are unrewarded by the market, whereas the things that we can be paid for are sometimes unfulfilling. If our work has the potential to serve others, it may take from us in the process. And, if we can find our true selves in our work, we can also lose ourselves in our work. The wrong work can literally kill us before we ever have a choice to do otherwise. The next few anecdotes are tragic tales of people who lost their lives for work-related reasons during the pandemic and come from conventional news sources, not "Those We've Lost." Surely, they, too, worked for a purpose but, without the context of their life stories to make sense of what they worked for and why, their deaths seem all the more senseless and tragic.

Workers who do not have the education and skills to choose work for anything more than material survival are vulnerable to abuse of power that infringes upon their basic human rights to health and safety. Nowhere was this more apparent during the pandemic than in the meat-packing industry, which was declared to be essential work in the United States to discourage the needless slaughter of animals raised solely to feed people. As famously documented in Upton Sinclair's *The Jungle*, meat-packing is dirty work, poorly paid, and historically, has employed and exploited immigrant labor. Such was the case more than a century later at Smithfield Foods, a meat processor where the coronavirus spread in close quarters on the factory floor and where Agustin Rodriguez Martinez was first known death. Even in good times, Martinez's job of disassembling pig carcasses was performed in dire conditions that were physically exhausting and mentally taxing. Toward the end, his wife reports that he was still mopping blood off the floor while running a fever from the virus that would claim his life.

Another essential line of work during the pandemic was the logistics industry that kept the supply of goods moving from factory to customer through contactless distribution channels. Later in the pandemic, even after Amazon had automated some roles previously performed by people, manual laborers at an Amazon distribution center were shocked to learn they were kept in the dark as they carried on with the urgency of production after one of their colleagues suffered a fatal heart attack on the job. The company disputed reports that, as employees continued to load and stack boxes, the area where the man's body lay was cordoned off by other boxes.

No work was more urgent during the pandemic than taking care of patients sick from the coronavirus, for which Lorna Breen was more prepared than most. A physician in a New York City hospital system that was overwhelmed by patients when the first wave of infections peaked, Dr. Breen had expected a crisis, and the staff around her marveled at her energy and organization as she worked with them to respond to the crisis. However, her contingency plans were upended when she contracted the virus herself, and while recovering, could barely empty her own dishwasher at home as she tried from afar to help manage a shortage of critical supplies at work. When she returned to work, the crisis had not abated, her energy had not returned, and the feeling of helplessness led her to refer to the experience as "the hardest time in my life." After Dr. Breen took her own life, a colleague remembered her saying, "I couldn't help anyone. I couldn't do anything. I just wanted to help people, and I couldn't do anything."

These extreme accounts of helplessness and despair concern workers who had no choice but to do the work they did or who did not believe they had a choice to do otherwise. Overwhelmed by economic conditions, managerial impositions, or personal motivations, the meaning and purpose of their work was overshadowed by its immediate urgency.

One final story from "Those We've Lost" suggests, more optimistically, that if our work lacks meaning and purpose, second chances are possible. Stuck pursuing conventional success in a dead-end career that he did not even realize he did not like, Robert Goolrick found meaning and purpose in his second career only after he was fired from his first. An advertising executive who learned to write as a copywriter, Mr. Goolrick drank too much while he worked on campaigns for champagne and beer. He later reflected that he had "no specific ambition" for the "talent and imagination" that enabled him to rise to leadership positions in multiple agencies. Rather, it was the material inducements of business achievement that kept him going. "My clothes were immaculate and my dinner parties a success, yet inside I felt completely dead." After he was pushed out of the New York City advertising business, he rediscovered his roots as a writer and southerner who was raised around too much alcohol and abuse. He reflected upon these experiences in a memoir that sold a modest 40,000 copies when it was published in his late 50's. That first book was to be a precursor to his eventual success as a bestselling novelist whose next book sold over 1 million copies. After so many years in the wrong career, he said that "writing about my life was a way of saving what's left."

Choosing Work with Meaning and Purpose

We hope that you are reading this book early enough in your working life that you are less concerned about saving what's left and more focused on seeking meaning and purpose in the work that's ahead. Few of us have a choice in the matter of whether to work. In fact, many of us will spend more of our adult lives working than doing practically anything else – enjoying hobbies, family time, relaxing, sleeping, or doing nothing at all. However, although we might not have the material freedom to choose *whether* to work, chances are that – by virtue of whatever led you to read this book – you do have a choice in the matter of *what work to do*. If you care about leading a life of meaning and purpose, then – as the foregoing stories suggest – work might play a significant part in supporting that objective or in getting in its way. It is worth considering what we owe to ourselves as *individual* actors seeking meaning and purpose.

At its best, your work has a chance to be your most meaningful contribution to the world. Most of us, however, will not make that contribution working alone, but rather by filling a function within an *organization* that enables us to participate in a production process that is bigger than ourselves. The work we contribute may come in the form of direct application of our skills and experience or by managing the work of others. If you are fortunate enough to be in a position in which your choices can influence the meaning and purpose of others' work, then it is worth considering what you owe to others.

Unfortunately, many people do not have sufficient motivation or energy to critically examine the meaning and purpose of their work or that of others. Rather, they accept their position in a marketplace that is largely beyond their individual capacity to control. They work within organizations that compete in a *system* that assigns a price to work as compensation for their misery and defines success as earning the greatest income in exchange for the least amount of effort.

The stories of pandemic victims are specific to a time and culture in which work perhaps meant something different than it means post-pandemic. They show us how work can define who we are and how work can take meaning away; they suggest that work can give us a reason to live but that work can also divert us from our purpose; and they depict the myriad forms of work that keep an economy moving forward but that, all too often, feel as if they don't matter at all. They also demonstrate the complexity of the terms "meaning," "purpose," and "work" – the central terms of this book that are also centrally important to anyone who works.

In Chapter 2, we will explore the theories and histories of these terms to understand what they mean, why they matter, and how studying stories from the past can serve a useful purpose as we contemplate the future. The central chapters of this book will consider the meaning and purpose of work at the three levels of analysis we just introduced – the individual, organization, and system – that are conventional in management scholarship and influential in management practice. In Chapters 3 and 4, we will examine in greater detail what work means to the *individuals* who perform it, taking into account their subjective perceptions that interact with their specific situations and roles. In Chapter 5, we will evaluate the potential obligations of *organizations* that have the opportunity to provide meaningful work to their employees or inhibit meaningful work entirely. In Chapter 6, we will see how the values of the *social and economic system* in which organizations operate and individuals work have the capacity to protect meaningful work or to put it in peril. Finally, in Chapter 7, we will glimpse into the future, taking stock of changes in work attitudes, workplaces, and working technologies – before this century and since the pandemic – to enable you to wonder about your own future and the future of work.

Questions and Prompts for Review and Reflection About Chapter 1

- What is the difference between thinking about meaning and purpose *prescriptively* and *descriptively*?
- Why do tragedies prompt reflection on the meaning and purpose of life and work?
- Interview someone who remembers working in the wake of the 9/11 attacks and/or during the COVID-19 pandemic. How did the events change their work? How did they change their thinking about the meaning and purpose of their work?
- What kind of work contributes the most to societal well-being (service to others)? What kind of work would you do if you could do anything you wanted (self-realization)? Could you earn a decent standard of living doing either of these things (market fit)? Why or why not?
- Overall, how do you feel about work: Does it give life meaning and purpose or does it detract from life's meaning and purpose?

Chapter 1 References

Banker, Steve. "Toilet Paper Shortages, Empty Shelves, and Panic Buying: Just How Bad Was Grocery Service in 2020?" *Forbes*. October 1, 2021. www.forbes.com/sites/stevebanker/2021/10/01/toilet-paper-shortages-empty-shelves-and-panic-buying-just-how-bad-was-grocery-service-in-2020/?sh=490b5dfd7b1a

BBC News. "Coronavirus: Armed Robbers Steal Hundreds of Toilet Rolls in Hong Kong." February 17, 2020. www.bbc.com/news/world-asia-china-51527043

Blustein, David L., and Paige A. Guarino. "Work and Unemployment in the Time of COVID-19: The Existential Experience of Loss and Fear." *Journal of Humanistic Psychology* 60, no. 5 (2020): 702–709. https://doi.org/10.1177/002216782093422

Care, Norman S. "Career Choice." *Ethics* 94, no. 2 (1984): 283–302.

Centers for Disease Control and Prevention. "CDC Museum COVID-19 Timeline." Accessed October 22, 2023. www.cdc.gov/museum/timeline/covid19.html

Chang, Alvin, Michael Sainto, Nina Lakhani, Rashida Kamal, and Aliya Uteuova. "The Pandemic Exposed the Human Cost of the Meatpacking Industry's Power: 'It's Enormously Frightening'." *The Guardian*. November 16, 2021. www.theguardian.com/environment/2021/nov/16/meatpacking-industry-covid-outbreaks-workers

Cho, Seung Jin, Jun Yeong Lee, and John V. Winters. "Employment Impacts of the Covid-19 Pandemic Across Metropolitan Status and Size." *Growth and Change* 52, no. 4 (2021): 1958–1996. https://doi.org/10.1111/grow.12540

Ciulla, Joanne B. *The Working Life: The Promise and Betrayal of Modern Work*. New York: Currency, 2001.

Collier, Peter. "How Covid Is Giving Rise to Kiosk Technology." *Supply Chain Brain*. November 11, 2021. www.supplychainbrain.com/blogs/1-think-tank/post/34008-how-the-pandemic-propelled-the-use-of-kiosk-technology

The Conference Board. "Survey: U.S. Job Satisfaction Hits All-Time High." May 11, 2023. www.conference-board.org/press/job-satisfaction-hits-all-time-high

Coolidge, Alexander. "P&G Largest U.S. Factory Making Charmin Toilet Paper Cleared to Stay Open." *Cincinnati Enquirer*. March 20, 2020. www.cincinnati.com/story/money/2020/03/20/p-g-largest-u-s-factory-making-charmin-toilet-paper-cleared-stay-open/2884161001/

Cottonelle. "The History of Toilet Paper." Accessed February 26, 2024. www.cottonelle.com/en-ca/tips-advice/toilet-paper-101/toilet-paper-history

Coyle, Diane. "Why Did It Take a Pandemic to Show How Much Unpaid Work Women Do?" *The New York Times*. June 26, 2020. www.nytimes.com/2020/06/26/opinion/sunday/inequality-gender-women-unpaid-work.html?

Cybersecurity & Infrastructure Security Agency. "Guidance on the Essential Critical Infrastructure Workforce." August 13, 2021. www.cisa.gov/resources-tools/resources/guidance-essential-critical-infrastructure-workforce

David, Jonathan, Shanara Visvalingam, and Melissa M. Norberg. "Why Did All the Toilet Paper Disappear? Distinguishing Between Panic Buying and Hoarding During COVID-19." *Psychiatry Research* 303 (2021): 114062. https://doi.org/10.1016/j.psychres.2021.114062

Day, Matt. "Amazon Is Running Out of Warehouse Workers. Cue the Robots." *Bloomberg*. December 6, 2022. www.bloomberg.com/news/features/2022-12-06/amazon-is-running-out-of-warehouse-workers-cue-the-robots

de Beauvoir, Simone. *The Ethics of Ambiguity*. Translated by Bernard Frechtman, 1949. Accessed February 26, 2024. www.marxists.org/reference/subject/ethics/de-beauvoir/ambiguity/

Ducharme, Jamie. "Why the COVID-19 Pandemic Has Caused a Widespread Existential Crisis." *Time*. December 29, 2020. https://time.com/5925218/covid-19-pandemic-life-decisions/

Dunklin, Reese, and Justin Pritchard. "$10 Toilet Paper? Coronavirus Gouging Complaints Surge in US." *The Associated Press*. March 19, 2020. https://apnews.com/article/virus-outbreak-health-us-news-ap-top-news-weekend-reads-53bf1ac57c50df34336c284bfe939212

Frankl, Viktor E. *Man's Search for Meaning*. New York: Pocket Books, 1985.

Georgieva, Krisalina, Stefania Fabrizio, Cheng Hoon Lim, and Marina M. Tavares. "The COVID-19 Gender Gap." *International Monetary Fund (IMF) Blog*. July 21, 2020. www.imf.org/en/Blogs/Articles/2020/07/21/blog-the-covid-19-gender-gap

Gilchrist, Karen. "Covid-19 Has Destroyed 22 Million Jobs in Advanced Countries, Says OECD." *CNBC*. July 7, 2021. www.cnbc.com/2021/07/08/oecd-covid-19-has-destroyed-22-million-jobs-in-advanced-countries.html

Goldberg, Emma. "All of Those Quitters? They're at Work." *The New York Times*. May 13, 2022. www.nytimes.com/2022/05/13/business/great-resignation-jobs.html

Gould, Elise, and Melat Kassa. "Low-Wage, Low-Hours Workers Were Hit Hardest in the COVID-19 Recession." *Economic Policy Institute*. May 20, 2021. www.epi.org/publication/swa-2020-employment-report/

Graeber, David. "Bullshit Jobs and the Yoke of Managerial Feudalism." *The Economist*. June 29, 2018. www.economist.com/open-future/2018/06/29/bullshit-jobs-and-the-yoke-of-managerial-feudalism

Greene, Kelly, and Carlos Tejada. "Workers Deeply Affected by Attacks Decide to Make Changes in Their Lives." *The Wall Street Journal*. December 26, 2001. www.wsj.com/articles/SB1009236905886354560

Gurchiek, Kathy. "What Are You Wearing While Working from Home?" *Society for Human Resource Management*. May 28, 2020. www.shrm.org/topics-tools/news/wearing-working-home

Harter, Jim. "Is Quiet Quitting Real?" *Gallup*, May 17, 2023. www.gallup.com/workplace/398306/quiet-quitting-real.aspx

Hume, Janice. "Portraits of Grief, Reflectors of Values: The New York Times Remembers Victims of September 11." *Journalism & Mass Communication Quarterly* 80, no. 1 (2003): 166–182. https://doi.org/10.1177/107769900308000111

Industrial Shredders. "How Toilet Paper Is Made – Basic Overview." November 10, 2015. www.industrialshredders.com/resources/how-toilet-paper-is-made-basic-overview

International Labour Organisation. *World Employment and Social Outlook 2023: The Value of Essential Work*, 2023. https://www.ilo.org/sites/default/files/wcmsp5/groups/public/@dgreports/@dcomm/@publ/documents/publication/wcms_871016.pdf

International Trade Administration. "Impact of COVID Pandemic on eCommerce." Accessed February 26, 2024. www.trade.gov/impact-covid-pandemic-ecommerce

Keynes, John Maynard. "Economic Possibilities for Our Grandchildren." In *Essays in Persuasion*, 358–373. New York: WW. Norton & Company, 1963.

Knoll, Corina, Ali Watkins, and Michael Rothfield. "'I Couldn't Do Anything: The Virus and an E.R. Doctor's Suicide." *The New York Times*. July 11, 2020. www.nytimes.com/2020/07/11/nyregion/lorna-breen-suicide-coronavirus.html

Leung, Janni, Jack Yiu Chak Chung, Calvert Tisdale, Vivian Chiu, Carmen C.W. Lim, and Gary Chan. "Anxiety and Panic Buying Behaviour During COVID-19 Pandemic – A Qualitative Analysis of Toilet Paper Hoarding Contents on Twitter." *International Journal of Environmental Research and Public Health* 18, no. 3 (2021): 1127. https://doi.org/10.3390/ijerph18031127

Lussenhop, Jessica. "Coronavirus at Smithfield Pork Plant: The Untold Story of America's Biggest Outbreak." *BBC News*. April 17, 2020. www.bbc.com/news/world-us-canada-52311877

Mao, Frances. "Coronavirus Panic: Why Are People Stockpiling Toilet Paper?" *BBC News*. March 4, 2020. www.bbc.com/news/world-australia-51731422

McKinsey Global Institute. "The Future of Work after COVID-19." February 18, 2021. www.mckinsey.com/featured-insights/future-of-work/the-future-of-work-after-covid-19

Michaelson, Christopher Wong, and Jennifer Tosti-Kharas. *Is Your Work Worth It? How to Think About Meaningful Work.* New York: PublicAffairs, 2024.

Mogg, Katie. "The 'Lazy-Girl Job' Is in Right Now. Here's Why." *The Wall Street Journal.* July 25, 2023. www.wsj.com/articles/the-career-goal-of-the-moment-is-a-lazy-girl-job-f5075c4e

Muirhead, Russell. *Just Work.* Cambridge, MA: Harvard University Press, 2007.

The New York Times. "Coronavirus World Map: Tracking the Global Outbreak." Accessed October 22, 2023. www.nytimes.com/interactive/2021/world/covid-cases.html

The New York Times. "Portraits of Grief." Accessed September 11, 2023. https://archive.nytimes.com/www.nytimes.com/interactive/us/sept-11-reckoning/portraits-of-grief.html

The New York Times. "Those We've Lost." Accessed February 26, 2024. www.nytimes.com/interactive/2020/obituaries/people-died-coronavirus-obituaries.html

Nozick, Robert. *The Examined Life: Philosophical Meditations.* New York: Simon & Schuster, 1990.

Oțelea, Marina Ruxandra, Agripina Rașcu, Cătălin Staicu, Lavinia Călugăreanu, Mădălina Ipate, Silvia Teodorescu, Ovidiu Persecă et al. "Exhaustion in Healthcare Workers after the First Three Waves of the COVID-19 Pandemic." *International Journal of Environmental Research and Public Health* 19, no. 14 (2022): 8871. https://doi.org/10.3390/ijerph19148871

Parker, Kim, and Juliana Menasce Horowitz. "Majority of Workers Who Quit a Job in 2021 Cite Low Pay, No Opportunities for Advancement, Feeling Disrespected." *Pew Research Center*, March 9, 2022. www.pewresearch.org/short-reads/2022/03/09/majority-of-workers-who-quit-a-job-in-2021-cite-low-pay-no-opportunities-for-advancement-feeling-disrespected/

Plato. *Apology.* Translated by Benjamin Jowett. Accessed February 26, 2024. www.gutenberg.org/files/1656/1656-h/1656-h.htm

Raifman, Julia, Alexandra Skinner, and Aaron Sojourner. "The Unequal Toll of COVID-19 on Workers." *Economic Policy Institute.* February 7, 2022. www.epi.org/blog/the-unequal-toll-of-covid-19-on-workers/

Ransome, Paul. *The Work Paradigm: A Theoretical Investigation of Concepts of Work.* Aldershot, Hants: Avebury, 1996.

Sainato, Michael. "'Lack of Respect': Outcry Over Amazon Employee's Death on Warehouse Floor." *The Guardian.* January 9, 2023. www.theguardian.com/technology/2023/jan/09/amazon-employee-death-warehouse-floor-colorado

Semuels, Alana. "Millions of Americans Have Lost Jobs in the Pandemic – And Robots and AI Are Replacing Them Faster Than Ever." *Time.* August 6, 2020. https://time.com/5876604/machines-jobs-coronavirus/

Sinclair, Upton. *The Jungle.* New York: Doubleday, 1906.

Solomon, Sheldon, Jeff Greenberg, and Tom Pyszczynski. "The Cultural Animal: Twenty Years of Terror Management Theory and Research." In *Handbook of Experimental Existential Psychology*, edited by Jeff Greenberg, Sander L. Koole, and Tom Pyszczynski, 13–34. New York: Guilford Press, 2004.

Toh, Michelle. "'It's Crazy': Panic Buying Forces Stores to Limit Purchases of Toilet Paper and Masks." *CNN Business.* March 6, 2020. www.cnn.com/2020/03/06/business/coronavirus-global-panic-buying-toilet-paper/index.html

Wieczner, Jen. "The Case of the Missing Toilet Paper: How the Coronavirus Exposed U.S. Supply Chain Flaws." *Fortune.* May 18, 2020. https://fortune.com/2020/05/18/toilet-paper-sales-surge-shortage-coronavirus-pandemic-supply-chain-cpg-panic-buying/

2 A Brief Overview of Meaning, Purpose, and Work

The Meaning of "Meaning"

Five months into his career at a management consulting firm, where it sometimes felt like it expected its people to be married to their work, Christopher married his wife. With three threadbare suits left over from his graduate student days, he decided to invest in a wedding suit that he could also wear in a workplace that required business attire at least four days a week. Finding nothing suitable for his build and budget in the New York department stores, he wandered into a nondescript Hong Kong clothier run by a family of Indian immigrants who called him, "boss." They measured him for the best-looking suit he would ever own – one that he then imagined announced to every power meeting he entered that he was a person of importance. However, the feature that was, for him, a special source of unexpected vanity was hidden on the inner left chest pocket, where his name was embroidered in cursive, golden thread.

That suit had meaning to him, in more ways than one. One sense of the meaning of "meaning" has to do with the meaning of words, or semantic meaning. The name in the suit referred to Christopher, and so, its presence signified that it belonged to him. If he took the suit coat off for an airplane flight and then it got mixed up with someone else's coat of similar color, pattern, and size, the name would serve as mutually acceptable evidence of which coat was his.

But, another sense of the meaning of meaning has to do with meaning in a less tangible but more significant sense. The embellishment of his name in golden thread felt, well, rich in a way that he'd never felt before. The only name on all of his previous clothes had been that of the designer who made them, not the person who wore them. The way in which the clothiers referred to him as "boss" contributed to his aura of self-importance. When he returned to his office in his new suit, he noticed that the security guards in his building also had *their* names inscribed on their uniforms in a similar style, only on the *outer* chest pocket. Whereas his hidden name was *psychologically* meaningful to him as the owner of his attire, their conspicuous names were *pragmatically* meaningful, indicating that they were there to serve, even

DOI: 10.4324/9781003307327-2

subserviently calling him "sir." When he emerged from the elevator into a meeting room, his name in his suit was a source of secret psychological strength, even as the cut and fabric of his suit conformed to the (spurious) advice of one of his mentors that to be powerful you must look powerful. In short, whereas the semantic meaning of his name on his suit was a sign that his suit *belonged to him*, he took the significant meaning of his name on his suit to communicate that *he belonged*.

If it is not already obvious from this narrative, in retrospect, Christopher feels somewhat sheepish that he cared so much when he was younger about social status, appearance, and the way in which appearance confers social status. The clothiers were experts at their craft and he was a novice in his, but they were also expert salesmen who called him "boss" not because he was important but because he had money. The security guards put their personal safety at risk in order to protect his safety, yet they called him "sir" because they were trained to flatter anyone who worked on a higher floor than they did. The language we use influences our perception of reality, and these examples of linguistic and nonlinguistic signification – the intentional or unintentional association of symbols with meaning – is ubiquitous in work and in professional life.

Historically, the colors of one's shirt collar communicated one's status as a blue-collar laborer, who worked with one's hands, or a white-collar professional, who purportedly worked with one's mind. Although the palette for work attire has proliferated in modern times, the metaphorical meanings of blue and white collar have endured, alongside the symbolic association of so-called "pink-collar" work with caring careers that was stereotypically women's work. At the world's most powerful power meeting, the World Economic Forum Annual Meeting in Davos, Switzerland, delegates' badge colors signify their level of access to a series of exclusive gatherings. Heads of state and top executives are allowed in spaces to which their staff and other sycophants are prohibited from entering. The colors not only signal to security guards whom to let in, but they are also a kind of shorthand for attendees themselves to determine in mixed company who is important enough with whom to mingle without having to stare conspicuously at someone else's name tag on their chest.

Both semantic and significant meaning posit a relationship between the signifier (the word, name, or sign) and the signified (the meaning of the word, name, or sign). Semantic meaning is, perhaps, the most familiar and basic form of meaning, often having to do with the meaning of words. The simplest way in which semantic meaning works is by relating a word in our language to a thing in our world, such as the way Christopher's name picks him out from other people who do not share his name, and in turn, designates him as the owner of a suit bearing his name. However, this form of meaning is actually not so simple at all. For one thing, other people share one, the other, or multiple parts of Christopher's name. His given name was one of the ten most popular boys' names in the United States the year he was born. His middle name, Wong, is one of the most common surnames in the world and yet differentiates him from all others who share his given name and surname, as far as he knows. So, the same word or word combination can have multiple meanings, or referents, as philosophers sometimes say. Moreover, semantic meaning does not always involve words; as we have seen, it can involve colors and other symbols that signify meanings that a community accepts as its code of operation. In different communities, the same sign can have different senses. So, for example, in Davos, green can mean entourage, which often communicates "stop them from entering" to a security guard, notwithstanding the nearly universal association elsewhere of green with "go."

Just as the same sign can have multiple referents, the same referent can have multiple names or signs. To some, Christopher is "boss," to others he is "sir," "professor," or "a**hole." His family has come up with infinite variations upon his name, and, depending upon the voice and intent with which they are used, the same name can have different senses – terms of endearment or annoyance. In this way, we can see how semantic meaning can also have significant meaning, implying through the use of linguistic terms and even the tone with which those terms are used whether the thing being named is *full of meaning* – someone who or something that matters.

Meaning and Meaningfulness

Ultimately, this book is about work that is *full of meaning*. We aim to cultivate readers' search for significant meaning in the work they pursue for themselves, perform for their employers, provide for their employees, and protect through the market and governmental policies that they promote. However, we cannot successfully pursue, perform, provide, produce, price, and protect meaningful work without a fundamental understanding of the semantic meaning of work – and of meaning, for that matter. We will explore the complex semantic and significant meaning of "work" later in this chapter, but first, we will reflect further on the difference between semantic and significant meaning of "meaning," or between "meaning" and "meaningful," if you will.

Two of the questions that might have occurred to you as you read about Christopher's wedding suit and the way workers from doormen to Davos display their names on their chests – questions that also occurred to us – include:

- Which meaning of Christopher's power suit is more meaningful: its signification of his professional status or its association with his wedding (which he considers to be, along with the births of his children, one of the most meaningful days of his life)?
- Whose work is more meaningful: the high rate per hour management consulting services Christopher provided in cities around the world wearing his power suit, the precision measurements performed by the New York-based custom clothiers selling suits on commission with whom

Christopher interacted, the fine stitching wrought by low wage-earning tailors in a Hong Kong factory who were all but invisible to their end user for whom they were handcrafting the suit, or the unionized security guards who spent all day, every day helping people find their way while keeping a watchful eye out for security threats?

Regardless of your answer, if you think it even makes sense to ask the first question, then you are at least receptive to the idea that not all meanings are equally meaningful. Whereas all meanings involve signification, only some signify something significant – or some significations are more significant than others. When his power suit was still new, Christopher wore it proudly with at least two meanings on his mind. One communicated outwardly to others about his professional status, and the other communicated inwardly to himself about his personal priorities.

Regarding professional status, part of the significant meaning of a suit is to communicate about social status. Wearing a suit is often uncomfortable and impractical – especially when traveling to clients during a humid Washington, DC summer – but it signified to those Christopher worked with that he was a knowledge worker whose toil took place in air-conditioned offices in which wool looked sharp, even in summertime. One function of a suit is to declare that those who wear them work with their heads, above the realm of pragmatic concerns that occupy those who work with their hands – such as carpenters and chefs, whose functional uniforms accommodate the tools of their trades.

The other part of the significant meaning of his suit to Christopher concerned personal priorities. When he was traveling for work, that suit was a personal and sentimental reminder of the married life that awaited him back home – one of the reasons for which he and his wife both worked, so they could build their future and family together.

Both questions – which meaning is more meaningful and which work is more meaningful – might seem to be matters of opinion. Subjectively, we might say that each kind of work – consulting, selling, sewing, and security – has a unique meaning to each different worker who performs it. For the professionally ambitious consultant, work can be a source of self-esteem, such that clients are willing to pay handsomely to fly the consultant in to solve their problems. For the personally sentimental consultant, those constant flights and long hours can become wearisome, justified by compensation that enables one to make a financial contribution to one's family's needs. Similarly, one tailor may see work as a means to the end of material survival, but another may see it as an opportunity to exercise creative and technical skills toward the production of a beautiful suit. In this way, meaning and meaningfulness are often said to be in the eye of the beholder.

However, whereas the first question suggests that some meanings may be taken to be meaningful and others not, the second question implies, further, that meaningfulness might occur in degrees from least to most meaningful.

One reaction you may have to each kind of work may, indeed, be subjective, based on your personal preferences for doing them. As you reflect, however, you may think beyond yourself to the kinds of values each type of work represents. In our prevailing capitalist system, management consulting is likely to be the most economically valuable of these forms of work, and sewing is likely to be the least, in terms of how much someone is willing to pay for each of these services; but economic value alone may not determine meaningfulness. You could make a case that security is the most socially valuable among these occupations, whether or not it is the most meaningful. Measuring customers and selling them suits demands a blend of social and economic skills, whereas sewing them requires creative acumen and craftsmanship. In economic markets, we often use economic value heuristically to designate professional prestige, but it takes only a moment's reflection to realize that there are many forms of meaningful work that do not pay well – and to think of high-paying professions that may strike us personally as meaningless. While this reflection may not yield definitive answers about which work is the most meaningful, it at least suggests different theories of value about meaningfulness that warrant our consideration – economic value, social value, and creative value, perhaps among many others. Which kind of work you consider to be most meaningful is likely to depend upon which theory or theories of value you subscribe to and in what order.

That is to say that, if there is a scale of meaning and meaningfulness that enables us to distinguish mere meaning from meaningfulness, less meaningful from more meaningful, and meaninglessness from meaningfulness, then we have reason to believe that meaningfulness is not purely in the eye of the beholder; that is, meaningfulness is not purely *descriptive*. From this perspective, meaningfulness is so in a *prescriptive* sense. This means that we should aspire to it not just because we like it but because we are right to like it.

The Foundations of Meaningfulness

To recap, meaning is semantic, and meaningfulness is significant. Meaning is multivalent – positive, negative, or neutral – whereas meaningfulness has positive valence, meaning that meaningfulness is generally a term of approval or aspiration. Both meaning and meaningfulness are open to subjective determination, but they are not subjectively determined. For example, with regard to semantic meaning, subjectively, the same work can mean different things to different people. One person might like to sell suits; another might prefer to sew them, and neither of them is necessarily wrong. However, it would be objectively wrong for somebody who does not share Christopher's name to take his suit coat because to do so would be to get the semantic meaning of his name wrong.

That seems straightforward enough, but unfortunately, we and many others who study meaning and meaningfulness are often undisciplined and use these terms interchangeably, even though the differences between them are both semantically and significantly different. For example, philosophers who have studied the meaning of life for thousands of years are actually studying what makes life meaning*ful* (or meaning*less*), but the title of the Monty Python film that pokes fun at this human search is, consistent with philosophers' parlance, *The Meaning of Life*. Similarly, social scientists who study the meaning of work are sometimes, as we shall see, interested in the different relationships – positive, negative, or neutral – people have to their work. However, they are often ultimately interested in what makes that work meaning*ful* – even though they profess to study the meaning of work. Full disclosure – we will often, as the book proceeds, follow convention in referring to the meaning of life and the meaning of work, even when we are really interested in what makes them meaning*ful*, and we trust that you will generally sense when we intend to imply one versus the other.

More important than getting the semantic meaning wrong, however, is getting significant meaning wrong. What does it mean to get significant meaning wrong – or, in other words, to be wrong about what is meaningful? The consequences of getting meaningfulness wrong might be much more profound than merely taking the wrong suit coat. In relation to work, they could include getting one's own priorities wrong, such as pursuing material wealth at the expense of other goods in life. This is not to say that wanting to be rich is always wrong, but it is to suggest that being rich is, perhaps, not the ultimate measure of how meaningful one's life is, even though it is, perhaps, the ultimate measure of one's market value. Being wrong about meaningful work might also consist in misplaced priorities about *others'* welfare. For example, Christopher does not actually know whether the Hong Kong tailors were celebrated artisans or poorly treated sweatshop workers who may not even have been located in Hong Kong. If we consider meaningful work to be a good worth pursuing for ourselves, we should also enable it for others who, chances are, would choose it for themselves if they had the material and moral freedom to do so.

And, for those fortunate enough to have the autonomy to choose their work, getting it wrong about meaningful work might also include choosing the wrong line of work, such as going into management consulting when one's destiny was to be a professor. This is not to imply that we regret our time in management consulting whatsoever because our time in that occupation prepared us for our respective moves into academe. The subjective fit between one's talents and interests is an important part of one's capacity to experience meaningful work. Although we both spent long hours in our management consulting days, we sometimes work longer hours as professors. No matter what your work, you may have to decide – or someone else may decide for you – about whether it is more necessary to spend another hour working or to allocate that hour to your family, your friends, or your other non-work pursuits. Getting it wrong means never getting that hour back to do something that might have been more meaningful than what you achieved at work.

The idea that life can have meaning is ultimately an optimistic proposal that our lives have lasting significance. When human beings throughout history have asked what is the meaning of life, they may have both wondered in this way whether it has any meaning at all, but arguably, more often, they have wondered with the purpose of discovering what it is so they can aspire to live more meaningfully. When they have wondered about what is the meaning of work, they have often settled for insignificant clichés like "There's a reason they call it work," a sign that work may be seen as detracting from the possibility of the meaningful life to which they aspire. The possibility of meaningful work suggests that work need not always detract from meaningful life – that work could serve as a means to the end of a meaningful life or even that work could be a significant part of what makes life meaningful.

Many of us will work the majority of our days for most of our adult lives, so the experience of meaningless or meaningful work will profoundly influence the overall possibility and experience of meaningful life. Sometimes, the calculation looks like working to live: In this narrative, work is not meaningful in itself, but it can be a means to the end of meaningfulness. That is to say that work enables us to survive materially, presumably the first step toward thriving meaningfully. If work does not leave us devoid of energy and enthusiasm to pursue meaningful endeavors outside of work – to socialize with the people who matter to us, to enjoy our recreational lives, to engage in creative projects, and so on – then it may be possible to achieve a healthy balance of non-meaningful work and meaningful life. While this balance may seem enticing, it is not always simple to determine what is enough material reward to support what is enough meaningful pursuit – and whether to seek that balance day to day or to sacrifice a portion of one's working life in hopes of an early retirement that may never come.

Other times, the calculation looks like living to work: In this narrative, work is a meaningful end in itself. But is it really more meaningful than the other endeavors that a commitment to one's work precludes – the personal relationships, the relaxation, the opportunity costs of putting meaningful work ahead of meaningful life? Whether working to live or living to work, the soundness of the calculation we make requires a theory of meaningfulness to justify it. If we forego professional advancement for the sake of more time at home, how do we know when we have used that time meaningfully – more meaningfully than we would have at the workplace? If we work longer hours for greater material rewards so that we can fund a slightly better lifestyle, how does a larger home or nicer clothes translate into more meaningfulness? If work is a means to more meaningful ends, we have to have a reason for believing those ends to be more meaningful than work. If work is an end in itself, we have to have a reason for believing in the meaningfulness of those ends.

But what is the theory of meaningfulness underlying these calculations? There have been, perhaps, as many theories of meaningfulness as there have been people, and as we have seen, it is, perhaps, easier to identify the risks of having an erroneous theory of meaningfulness than to pick out the right one. Philosophers, too, disagree in their definitions of meaningfulness – they even disagree about the possibility of meaningfulness – but among those who have seriously studied the meaning of life, many agree that meaningfulness exists at the intersection of the good, the true, and the beautiful. This does not answer the question of how much of each is required of meaningfulness and whether they exist in a certain order of priority, but it does help us to understand how we might prioritize.

So, for example, if we return to the question of which work is most meaningful – that of consulting, selling, sewing, or security – we can make a case for each. We may understand "the good" to be a proxy for social value, or how helpful one's work is to society, which puts the security guard's work in a meaningful light. "The true" could be taken to be a measure of economic value, prioritizing the work of the consultant or the seller. "The beautiful" may be measured in terms of aesthetic value created by the tailors. In this context, we can see that we can make a case for the meaningfulness of all of these forms of work, though we have not yet answered definitively whether some are more meaningful than others and why.

The Meaning of 'Work'

When we talk about the *meaning* of work, we tend to presuppose that we know the meaning of '*work*.' However, much as the meaning of 'meaning' is complicated by the question "meaning to whom?", the meaning of 'work' is complicated by the question, "work to whom?"

In the famous whitewashing scene from Mark Twain's novel, *The Adventures of Tom Sawyer*, the titular character is overcome by a "deep melancholy" as he surveys the work before him on an otherwise beautiful weekend afternoon: "Thirty yards of board fence nine feet high" that his Aunt Polly has required him to paint – punishment for provoking a fight with a new boy in town and then sneaking home well past his bedtime. As any of us can relate to when confronted with a mountain of work in which we have no interest, "Life to him seemed hollow, and existence but a burden."

Much folk wisdom seems to resonate with this fictional passage that so accurately captures a familiar attitude about work. Putative truths concerning work include, for example, the claim, "A bad day fishing is better than a good day at work." In *Tom Sawyer*, kids skip out on school to go fishing, they go missing because they're whiling away the time fishing, and they imagine running away from their chores and schoolwork at home to a life of freedom that will be spent fishing. In modern life, vendors sell t-shirts, wall plaques, key chains, and other memorabilia declaring the bearer's relative enthusiasm for fishing over work, including, appropriately, a fishing hat. If fishing is not your jam, there is also a robust industry in nearly identical accessories that substitute the words 'golfing,' 'sewing,' or just about anything other than 'working' for 'fishing,' suggesting that a good day at work is worse than a bad day at almost anything else.

The point of this alleged insight is less about our particular preferences for play than it is about our supposed universal derision of work. On this view, even a good day at work pales in comparison to pointless play, but the problem lurking beneath the slogan is that play is but a temporary escape from the sentence to work that will inevitably recapture us with the mandate of necessity. Tom Sawyer's solution to that problem invokes another simplistic saying about work that you may have heard, "Do what you love and you'll never work a day in your life." This paradoxical command suggests, at the same time, that work should be avoided, and yet, it is unavoidable, so you might as well seek work that doesn't feel like work. As anyone who has ever tried to follow this advice has discovered, the problem is that to do what you love for a living is far easier said than done.

Tom's ingenious way of finding work that he loves is to pretend so ardently that he loves the work that he actually despises that the neighborhood children who are walking past while he whitewashes wonder about what has him so enraptured. As Ben Rogers comes skipping past, Tom pretends to be engrossed in painting so as not to notice him, leading Ben to slow down to ask what Tom is working on. Tom says, "What do you call work?" to which Ben replies, "Well, ain't *that* work?" to which Tom responds, in turn, "Well, maybe it is, and maybe it ain't. All I know is, it suits Tom Sawyer." This declaration of suitability entices Ben to ask to test whether whitewashing suits him too, which Tom grants in exchange for Ben's half-eaten apple. By the end of the afternoon, Tom has manipulated his friends into applying three coats of paint to the fence and is "literally rolling in wealth" with the apple, a kite, a tin soldier, and other bounty that he extracts from others in exchange for their chance to do his work for him.

Reflecting upon his day in which he recruited and capitalized upon a team of laborers to perform a project that he managed, "Tom said to himself that it was not such a hollow world, after all." Meanwhile, the narrator suggests that work – like meaning is sometimes alleged to be – is in the eye of the beholder. The chapter concludes, "If he had been a great and wise philosopher . . . he would now have comprehended that Work consists of whatever a body is obliged to do, and that Play consists of whatever a body is not obliged to do."

Glib though Twain's definition of work might be, it is awfully similar to that of the great and wise philosopher, Aristotle. The ancient Greek thinker characterized work as that which was done to enable leisure. In other words, work is a necessary means to the end of that which is an unnecessary end in itself. In Aristotle's era – as in Tom Sawyer's pre-Civil War America and in our world today – necessary work was often delegated to servants and slaves, allowing people of Aristotle's caste to play at the comparatively noble endeavor of philosophical contemplation. Enticing as this simple meaning of work might be, it probably provokes as many questions about what counts as work as it provides answers. As a case in point, it is ambiguous about the activity that engages us at this very moment – writing a book about work that may not be strictly necessary but that, at the same time, hardly feels like we are at play. David Graeber coined the term "bullshit jobs" to characterize work, the point of which is primarily to keep people busy without actually making a meaningful difference in the world. To us, writing this book doesn't feel like bullshit either, but then you, the reader, are probably a better judge of that than we are.

The question "work to whom?" implies that there is an inescapable element of subjectivity to what is work and what is necessary. As a philosophical matter, the question suggests that work is a state of mind – to the individual doing it and their inclination to do it and to the individuals around the worker who do or do not need it to be done. As a practical matter, however, the activity that we call 'work' is not only a subjective state of mind but also an objective phenomenon that is or is not recognized as such by the state. Formal recognition not only confers status on certain forms of work over others but also renders it eligible for minimum compensation and subjects it to the state's regulatory and economic scrutiny. In his 1996 book, *The Work Paradigm*, social theorist Paul Ransome sets out several objective criteria of work as an institutional phenomenon, not just an individual feeling. These criteria characterize work as "purposeful expedient activity" that "requires mental and/or physical exertion," "carried out in exchange for wages or salary" as "a public activity" and "recognized as work for 'official purposes' such as taxation and insurance." However, just as Aristotle's simple account of work left room for ambiguity, Ransome's complex criteria are also problematic, seeming to exclude from the category of work some very important forms of work, such as caring for one's own children, that have historically been undervalued – and, perhaps not coincidentally, that have historically fallen disproportionately upon women.

These attempts to specify the meaning of 'work' signify that how we objectively define work is subjectively influenced by what we value, and how we objectively value work is influenced by how we subjectively define it. In *Is Your Work Worth It?*, we define work as "purposeful, effortful, and recognized" by society as work. Notably, however, objective recognition usually comes in the form of a tax authority determining whether work is taxable, but subjectively, we often experience untaxed purposeful effort as work. For example, is Tom's whitewashing work, even though Aunt Polly is punishing him with it rather than paying him for it? If punishment were the purpose of work, then of course, we would recoil from it, a case in point illustrating how our work values are influenced by how we define work and vice versa. Alternatively, did Aunt Polly conveniently choose whitewashing as Tom's work chore because the fence happened to be in disrepair? We cannot say with certainty whether restoring the fence is a purpose that would have definitively changed Tom's perception of his task, but it does suggest that the same work can mean different things depending upon the reason it is perceived to be work.

In addition to what work is, other questions that we should ask about work pertain to who, what, why, when, and so on. Who does it? The status of work as work may differ, depending upon whose responsibility it is to perform it. If Aunt Polly does the work around her own home, is it work in the same way that it would be if she found a hired hand to do it for her? For whom is it done? Would it make a difference in the necessity of the work if the fence that belongs to Aunt Polly, instead, belonged to the city as an historic landmark, like the real fence in Hannibal, Missouri today with a plaque that says, "Tom Sawyer's Fence"? If the hired hand is a professional rather than her nephew, for what, in return, are they doing it? Does the status of work as work change if it is being performed by Tom as punishment versus being performed by a hired hand for pay? Is it still work if the neighborhood children are paying Tom for the privilege of performing it? "How much?" is another related question. Does the amount of pay determine the status of whether it is work or the prestige of the work – for example, if Aunt Polly hires a jack-of-all-trades who works for a modest hourly wage versus an artisan painter who commands a premium? When is it done? Part of Tom's melancholy is provoked by the fact that it is Saturday – a traditional day of rest and play, not work. Does weekend work count as work? How about where it is done? Painting is a physical task that is ordinarily performed at the location of the painted object. The modern privilege of remote work applies more to work of the mind than to work of the body, invoking the question of how. How is the work done? Tom's mindful work of managing the project ultimately earns him far more in wealth than laboring as a painter would have done. Work of the mind multiplies the number of hands that can engage in a project, whereas work of the body can only be done with a laborer's own two hands.

Any definition of work consists of answers to all these questions – Why? Who? For whom? For what in return? How much in return? When? Where? How? And so on. Each worker's personal definition of work reveals what they value, at the same time as what they value is revealed by how they answer these questions.

While our individual definitions of work both manifest and reflect our values, work can also manifest and reflect institutional values. Imagine, for example, that Aunt Polly represents not only Tom's aunt but Tom's institutional employer – say, Aunt Polly's Painted Exteriors. Her use of work to punish her employees will influence their experience of work as something to begrudge. By contrast, if we imagine Tom as the proprietor of Tom Sawyer's Painted Exteriors, his laborers – who have paid for the privilege of a piece of the painting job – are more likely to regard themselves as customers and to wear hats and t-shirts sporting the phrase "A bad day painting is better than a good day at work." They would not see painting as work at all.

Philosopher Joanne Ciulla and sociologist Russell Muirhead have observed how attitudes toward work have evolved through history, manifesting and reflecting not just individual and organizational values but also societal values. They both utilize the phrase "curse to calling" to describe the gradual progression, at least in Western society, of work as a curse to be avoided to a calling to be embraced. The perspective on work as a curse is demonstrated in, for example, the ancient Greek democracy in which the elites who had full citizenship rights performed the mindful work of running the government, while their servants and slaves did the dirty work. Aristotle's perspective on perfect happiness as consisting of philosophical contemplation is the exemplification of an attitude that the life of the mind was not only superior to the life of labor but also all the purer the less labor it deigned to involve. Most historians of work identify the Reformation as an inflection point in the progression from curse to calling, when economic capitalism was taking hold in industrializing society and expanding political rights rendered it less possible for a growing middle class to rely exclusively upon the toil of a laboring underclass. In his seminal book *The Protestant Ethic and the Spirit of Capitalism*, sociologist Max Weber observed that religious leaders recast both mindful and manual work as an earthly calling to justify the satisfaction of material needs, infusing the "work ethic" with an inherent dignity and purpose.

We don't presume to have captured the full force of historical attitudes toward work in a single paragraph, but we think the historical observations of others warrant mention here for at least two reasons. First, we believe that there is some truth to the historical claim that, as society has gradually democratized over time, changing attitudes toward work from a necessity that privileged people should avoid to a necessity that is unavoidable for nearly all people has led us to regard work as potentially both necessary and noble. Second, our own observations of very recent history suggest that the consideration of work as a potential calling is near its peak. As we will explore in more detail in Chapter 3, not only is rhetoric about finding one's calling palpable in the present during which we are writing this book, but the very phrase "work as a calling" has exponentially increased in usage over the past century.

At the same time, the reason we have not given more than a paragraph to the historical evolution of work from curse to calling is that we believe that this historical account, like all history, cannot avoid being a convenient story that is quite a bit more complex than that if we were to delve into the details. The historians do not say that everyone who worked in ancient Greece was cursed, nor do they contend that everyone who works in the modern world has a calling. Aristotle, himself, who lived and extolled the life of the mind, arguably would have experienced work as a calling if he considered philosophy and politics to be work, which he did not. Tom Sawyer, who used his clever mind to avoid physical work, might have experienced managing the work of others, which Ransome's definition of work considers to be work, to be play. As we will explore in Chapter 6, essential workers during the COVID-19 pandemic were called to serve, though not all of them felt called from the inside to the work. And so, we concur with the historians that the societal forces around us influence values and attitudes toward work at the same time as we contend that those values and attitudes toward work influence what we as a society institutionalize, recognize, reward, and tax as work. The meaning of 'work,' like the meaning of 'meaning,' is neither solely in the eye of the beholder nor immune to the perception of the beholder but rather in the intersection between them.

"Meaning," "Purpose," and the Purpose of Work

A famous parable of a stonemason building a cathedral is intended to illustrate the power of working for a higher purpose. The story, which has ambiguous origins, involves two stonemasons in its simplest telling. One, when asked what he is doing, says simply that he is cutting and laying down stone. The other proclaims proudly that he is building a cathedral. In one variation on the story, the former looks with downcast eyes while complaining that his back aches, and the latter spreads his arms wide while looking skyward. In another version, there are three stonemasons: the first still complains about his work, the second accepts his work because it supports his family, and the third embraces his work because it celebrates God. In any telling of the tale, we are led to presume that the stonemason with a higher purpose is a better craftsman, a harder worker, and a happier human being. A modern retelling alleges that, when United States President John F. Kennedy visited National Aeronautics and Space Administration facilities, a custodian he encountered declared that he was putting a man on the moon.

The moral of working with a sense of purpose stands in stark contrast to another old tale – the myth of Sisyphus – in which the former king of Ephyra was punished by the gods for cheating death, sentenced for eternity to repeatedly roll a boulder up a hill that inevitably would roll down again. The philosopher Richard Taylor characterizes Sisyphus' life as the quintessence of "endless pointlessness," the existentialist Albert Camus used Sisyphus' story as the archetype of the absurd, and "Sisyphean" has come to be an adjective used by office workers and manual laborers alike to describe the way we often feel about working without a point and purpose. Studs Terkel's 1972 collection of interviews, *Working*, in which "people talk about what they do all day and how they feel about what they do," proves that both the stonemason and Sisyphus are symbols of real people. Steelworker Mike Lefevre dreams of pointing up at the Empire State Building and telling his son, "See, that's me over there on the forty-fifth floor. I put the steel beam in." Meanwhile, telephone receptionist Sharon Atkins says of her repetitive toil, "you're just a little machine. A monkey could do what I do. It's really unfair to ask someone to do that." More than 50 years later, many receptionists – workers who answered telephones and took messages for their bosses who were too busy to answer their own telephones – have, in fact, been replaced by machines.

Why does purpose matter? As we have already seen, some social scientists who have studied how people experience meaning and purpose in life have postulated that one impulse for the pursuit of purpose is terror management, meaning that the idea of a life that leaves no permanent trace is too terrifying to accept. This prospect has led theologians to point to following God's plan as the source of ultimate purpose in life, whereas secular philosophers have sought to locate ultimate purpose in the legacies we leave behind, made problematic when our attempts to live on through the memories of others are threatened by the eventual dissolution of the universe. But would you rather be remembered in the hearts and minds of your loved ones, knowing that they too will someday perish, and with them, their recollections of you, or by generations of people unknown to you who benefit from your inventions that made their lives better? The fact of work complicates the legacy we wish to leave: Ideally, we would like to live on in both ways and not to have to choose between them, but realistically, the choice to invest more time in our professional achievements typically leaves less time for our personal lives.

In relation to art, philosopher Immanuel Kant defined purpose as "the object of a concept insofar as we regard this concept as the object's cause." This seems like an especially complicated way of saying that purpose is the effect of a cause. The ancient Greek philosopher Aristotle similarly referred to the final cause of any entity, whether a natural phenomenon or a human creation, as its *telos*, or purpose. Purpose is the answer to the question, "Why?" or "What for?"

However, as we have already seen, the same work can have multiple purposes, as the same cause can have multiple effects. One stonemason who perceives his work as the task of cutting and laying down stone is, perhaps, not wrong about its *functional purpose*, but the other who sees the end goal of this work as the construction of a cathedral in supplication to a divine order is focused on a so-called higher or *moral purpose*. When Ransome characterizes work as "purposeful expedient activity . . . for 'official purposes' such as taxation and insurance," he is focusing on sociological criteria that enable a community to share a conception of what counts as work. However, the subjective experience of work may include the psychological sense that one's work is more than its descriptive function. In the parlance of meaning, we might think of functional purpose as, akin to semantic meaning, an empirical description of the work, whereas moral purpose is akin to meaningfulness, imbuing the same activity with significant meaning.

In business, the functional purpose of work has long been presumed to be to make a profit. Milton Friedman's famous edict that "the social responsibility of business is to increase its profits" implies also that the more profit, the better. Whereas ethical debate about shareholder value maximization has focused on the tradeoffs between money and the moral rights of other stakeholders whose loss may be investors' gain, we also propose a tension between the functional purpose of profit and the possibility that business could serve a higher purpose. From this perspective, it is not wrong to acknowledge that business must make a profit to stay in business but to assert profit as the ultimate purpose of business is to confuse cause and effect, means and ends, meaning and meaningfulness. Profit is not the reason for being of business any more than making the most money is the ultimate end of human work.

We prefer an optimistic reason to pursue meaning and purpose at work and in life. Like many philosophers through the ages, we believe that the pursuit of meaning and purpose is integral to what it means to be human. No matter what our belief system may be, we tend to agree that there is something precious and fragile about our temporary time on this Earth and that there are better and worse options for deciding how to spend that time. Proponents of a YOLO (You Only Live Once) movement agree on living life to the fullest but disagree on the place of work in a full life. If work must occupy much of our time, it stands to reason that we ought to optimize our time at work in ways that cultivate the best kind of life. However, it is not trivial to decide whether we should work to live, live to work, whether we should seek Financial Independence to Retire Early (the FIRE movement), or whether we should work without concern for the financial return as long as our salary satisfies our material needs, whether we should work hard to play hard, and so on. This optimistic view suggests that work has the potential to be a primary force that *enables us* to pursue meaning and purpose in our lives. More than likely, there is reason for both pessimism and optimism about the way that work interacts with meaning and purpose. It may depend upon the person, the job, the circumstances, the timing, the reasons we have, the way we work, and the rewards for which we work, and so on – who, what, where, when, why, how, and how much, among other questions.

But how do meaning and purpose relate to each other? Some people – even professional philosophers – treat them as though they are one and the same, but more often, the question of how they relate is glossed over. We think it is important enough to consider this question that we included both terms in the title of our book and have made conscious choices about when to use meaning, purpose, or both. Our perspective is that they are different enough that it is possible to have meaning without purpose or purpose without meaning, but they are close enough that often meaning confers a sense of purpose or purpose confers a sense of meaning.

For example, think back to the Hong Kong tailors to whom the creation of Christopher's suit was outsourced. Christopher never met them, but at the same time that he optimistically imagined that they worked in a fashion haven in which they luxuriated in precious fabrics, he worried and wondered whether they toiled away in the kinds of coercive sweatshops that are all too common in the garment industry. As Immanuel Kant suggests with the phrase "purposiveness without purpose," the experience of something beautiful may be all the more meaningful when it is disconnected from any discernible functional purpose. Conversely, making clothes for money has a functional purpose without necessarily having significant meaning.

Yet, work that is meaningful to us can make us feel purposeful, as in the case of Christopher's first job out of graduate school. Every time he got on an airplane to visit a client in another city, he had mixed feelings that he was leaving home but that, in his father's eyes, he knew enough that somebody in another city was willing to pay for him to fly there to advise them. Similarly, the story of the stonemason building a cathedral suggests that aspiring to a higher purpose is more meaningful than merely framing one's work as a manual task.

These examples reinforce the teleological nature of purpose, meaning that it involves a journey toward a destination, or *telos*, whereas meaningfulness can be discovered in the moment, at rest, or at any other point along that journey. In management scholarship and practice, we have observed that meaning and meaningfulness are more often attributed to individuals' experience of work, whereas purpose is more often associated with an organization's reason for being. This is not a strict practice, however; Christopher's former consulting firm used to entice its staff to consider the alignment between their individual purpose and the purpose of the organization. We are not aiming to settle once and for all the question of how meaning and purpose relate, but rather to have a consistent approach to our use of them that works for our readers. They overlap but are not coextensive with each other.

Meanwhile, our three central concepts (meaning, meaningfulness, and purpose) are complemented by three intersecting levels of analysis that we will explore in the next three chapters: individuals, organizations, and systems or society. Individuals perform work but typically do so within organizations. Organizations compete with one another in a market system. And that market system is sanctioned by a social agreement that the market ought to serve the needs and wants of the individuals within it. Business constitutes an environment in which much work is done, but there is work outside of business. All of which is to say that none of this is simple, but all of it is worth thinking about and acting upon. In summary, the purpose of the work we have done in this chapter has been to introduce the meaning of the three central concepts of this book – meaning, work, and purpose – toward the ultimate goal of enabling our readers to consider the meaning and purpose of their work.

Questions and Prompts for Review and Reflection About Chapter 2

- Think of an object that is meaningful to you (for example, a gift you received from someone you care about or a certificate or medal that you earned). Try to identify it to someone else purely in terms of its *semantic* meaning. Then add an explanation of what makes it *significant* (i.e., meaningful) to you.
- Think about two people who have the same occupation yet feel very differently about its meaningfulness – or better yet, interview them. What does this tell you about the possibility that meaningfulness can be *subjective* (i.e., in the eye of the beholder)?
- Reflect upon the occupation in the foregoing question. What are some *objective* reasons why that type of work is meaningful – or meaningless?
- Do you aspire to work to live or to live to work? Why? How does your answer to this question depend upon your definition of work and whether it is a curse or calling?
- Think about an activity that you partake of on a regular basis (it can be your job if you have one, or it can be a sport, an artistic endeavor, or even a game). What is the *functional* purpose of the activity and what is its *moral* (i.e., higher) purpose (if any)?

Chapter 2 References

Brennan, Tad. "Telos." In *Routledge Encyclopedia of Philosophy*. London: Taylor and Francis. www.rep.routledge.com/articles/thematic/telos/v-1

Camus, Albert. *The Myth of Sisyphus*. Translated by Justin O'Brien. New York: Vintage Books, 1961.

Carton, Andrew M. "'I'm Not Mopping the Floors, I'm Putting a Man on the Moon: How NASA Leaders Enhanced the Meaningfulness of Work by Changing the Meaning of Work." *Administrative Science Quarterly* 63, no. 2 (2018): 323–369. https://doi.org/10.1177/0001839217713748

Ciulla, Joanne B. *The Working Life: The Promise and Betrayal of Modern Work*. New York: Currency, 2001.

Estes, Adam Clark. "A Visual Guide to the Many Different Davos Badges." *Atlantic*. January 18, 2012. www.theatlantic.com/international/archive/2012/01/visual-guide-many-different-davos-badges/332913/

Frege, Gottlob. "Sense and Reference." *Philosophical Review* 57, no. 3 (May 1948): 209–230. https://doi.org/10.2307/2181485

Friedman, Milton. "A Friedman Doctrine: The Social Responsibility of Business Is to Increase Its Profits." *The New York Times*. September 13, 1970. www.nytimes.com/1970/09/13/archives/a-friedman-doctrine-the-social-responsibility-of-business-is-to.html

Graeber, David. "Bullshit Jobs and the Yoke of Managerial Feudalism." *The Economist*. June 29, 2018. www.economist.com/open-future/2018/06/29/bullshit-jobs-and-the-yoke-of-managerial-feudalism

Jones, Terry (Director). *Monty Python's The Meaning of Life*, 1983. www.imdb.com/title/tt0085959/

Kant, Immanuel. *Critique of the Power of Judgment*. Translated by Paul Guyer and Eric Matthews. Cambridge: Cambridge University Press, 2000.

Metz, Thaddeus. *Meaning in Life: An Analytic Study*. Oxford: Oxford University Press, 2013.

Michaelson, Christopher Wong, and Jennifer Tosti-Kharas. *Is Your Work Worth It? How to Think About Meaningful Work*. New York: PublicAffairs, 2024.

Muirhead, Russell. *Just Work*. Cambridge, MA: Harvard University Press, 2007.

Ransome, Paul. *The Work Paradigm: A Theoretical Investigation of Concepts of Work*. Aldershot, Hants: Avebury, 1996.

Smart, J.J.C. "Meaning and Purpose." *Philosophy Now* 24, no. 16 (1999): 16. https://philosophynow.org/issues/24/Meaning_and_Purpose

Solomon, Sheldon, Jeff Greenberg, and Tom Pyszczynski. *The Worm at the Core: On the Role of Death in Life*. New York: Random House, 2015.

Sonday, Laura. "Examining the Economic Tether and the Meaning of Work." Dissertation submitted to University of Michigan, 2021. https://doi.org/10.7302/3048

Taylor, Richard. *Good and Evil*. New York: Macmillan, 1970.

Terkel, Studs. *Working: What People Do All Day and How They Feel About What They Do*. New York: Pantheon Books, 1974.

Twain, Mark. *The Adventures of Tom Sawyer*. Berkeley: University of California Press, 1980.

Weber, Max. *The Protestant Ethic and the Spirit of Capitalism*. New York: Dover, 2003.

Wolf, Susan. *Meaning in Life and Why It Matters*. Princeton, NJ: Princeton University Press, 2010.

3 Meaningful Work for Individuals

Jobs, Careers, and Callings

From Meaningless to Meaningful Work

Sisyphus, the character from Ancient Greek mythology mentioned in the previous chapter, was doomed to the eternally purposeless chore of rolling a boulder up a hill only for it to roll down again and remains a potent symbol of meaningless work. That pattern has been repeated in workplaces across time, from the opening pages of Adam Smith's *The Wealth of Nations* – in which assembly line workers manufacturing pins perform the same narrow tasks, over and over again – to David Foster Wallace's *The Pale King* – in which tax examiners entertain suicidal thoughts while pushing endless piles of paper. So many forms of meaningless work exist that anthropologist David Graeber posits that easily one-half of so-called "bullshit jobs" could go away with no marked negative impact on society. Included on Graeber's list of such jobs – and doubtless on our own personal lists of jobs we would prefer *not* to have, all else being equal – are telemarketers. The daily work of "cold-calling" unsuspecting people in their homes, at what will certainly be an inopportune hour; delivering a preset spiel, complete with branching conversational logic matched to the level of indignation on the receiving end of the call; and measuring success by ultimately convincing another person to agree to something they weren't previously imagining, likely involving financial expenditures in line with the goals of one's employer combines much of what defines a typically meaningless job.

So embedded in the cultural zeitgeist is our collective disdain for the drudgery of telemarketing that musician and activist Boots Riley, himself a former telemarketer, set his 2018 film, *Sorry to Bother You*, in a call center. Riley is a devout anti-capitalist who believes workers should democratically control the wealth created by their labor, and the film is an unflinching, albeit surreal, portrayal of the perils of late-stage capitalism. Not only is the protagonist, Cassius "Cash" Green, put in a drab cubicle, infantilized with trite corporate slogans and incentives, and surveilled by management during his calls, but when he calls people, the film shows him literally crashing through the wall into their apartments – a move Riley says was meant to illustrate the deep personal intrusion such calls typically represent. A severe blow comes

DOI: 10.4324/9781003307327-3

when Cash, who is Black, is instructed by a well-meaning Black co-worker to "use your white voice . . . like being pulled over by the police" to appeal to the presumably majority White audience on the receiving end of the calls. In fact, this sonorific change – which, in the film, is literally voiced by a different, White actor – appears to reverse Cash's fortunes and propel him to being one of the most successful salespeople in the company. The film makes clear that success accompanies an ability to roll with the various indignities required of the job, compromising one's own racial identity among them. What this cuttingly satirical portrayal of work also makes clear is that Cash becomes effective not when the work is made more meaningful, but rather the opposite. His success comes when work is trivialized to the point of being absurd – even more so in a final plot twist that we would not want to spoil here but is well worth the ride – and he leans into it, perhaps accepting that resistance is futile if one is to survive in the corporate world.

All of this begs the question: Is it fair to describe telemarketing – or any occupation – as truly meaningless? What makes it so? Is there something about *work itself* that makes it such drudgery? Organizational psychologists Richard Hackman and Greg Oldham developed a theoretical model proposing the "job characteristics" that contribute to positive attitudes and behaviors among employees. The idea behind this model is that there are elements of how the job is designed – elements that managers can reasonably control – that contribute to or detract from employee engagement, performance, and commitment. Telemarketing, as it turns out, typically combines many of the factors that contribute to worse outcomes: The work is repetitive, requiring the same skills and often a set script to read, rather than allowing workers to demonstrate a variety of skills; there is a lack of personal autonomy and control over when, where, and how the work gets done (see again the script); and critically, there is typically no recognition by others or society that the work is important. In fact, the telemarketer is more likely to receive feedback on their efforts via the sound of a slamming phone, an expletive, or worse. One can imagine this work being demoralizing, and that is exactly what job characteristics theory would predict. These elements of job design – autonomy, control, recognition – reduce the *task significance* of the work; that is, it decreases the *subjective meaningfulness* of the work. In turn, lower task significance is linked to a host of negative outcomes for workers and their organizations, including reduced motivation, poorer quality performance, lower job satisfaction and commitment, and higher turnover. An important assumption behind job characteristics theory is that, because managers can control elements like how much autonomy employees have, how much skill variety the work entails, and how much feedback employees receive, they have the opportunity to design interventions that can essentially boost the meaningfulness of the work. Philosophers like Adina Schwartz assert that employers have a *prescriptive obligation* to provide employees the opportunity for autonomy, control, and recognition, among other moral goods. In addition, Hackman and Oldham suggest that employers stand to enjoy the "downstream" attitudinal and performance benefits of enhancing their employees' experience of task significance in the form of profitable rewards. Or, like the bosses in *Sorry to Bother You*, they can ignore this opportunity to the detriment of themselves and society (but no spoilers).

It seems important, then, to pose yet another question: Can even a seemingly meaningless job like telemarketing be made marginally more meaningful for those performing it? Research by organizational psychologist Adam Grant provides a novel entry point into this question. Grant and his co-authors studied a specific type of telemarketer: a college student earning money by calling alumni to solicit donations. While perhaps the sense of shared identity and camaraderie inherent in having the marketers attend the same university as their marks might make this job appear less intimidating than the typical telemarketing hustle, an unsolicited sales call is still an unsolicited sales call. Those on the receiving end of such calls might experience thoughts along the lines of, "How many years of my tuition money did this institution already devour; how dare they ask for more?" In fact, Jen knows someone who created a setting in their phone to automatically send calls from their former university's area code and prefix directly to voicemail. Against this discouraging backdrop, Grant and a team of researchers undertook a study with an ambitious goal: to design an intervention to increase the motivation of student call center workers. They believed this goal might be achieved through tapping into the positive impact the work had on others, in the form of a five-minute meeting between callers and the fellow students who had received the scholarships their calls funded. As it turned out, this brief meeting had a profound effect: Callers spent almost 1.5 times as long on the phone and raised 1.7 times more money when they had been randomly assigned to meet with the scholarship awardees than the control groups who did not meet the students. Grant attributes these outcomes to "prosocial motivation". Contact with the beneficiaries of the work increased the sense that their work made a difference, which, in turn, enhanced how meaningful the work felt, which, *in turn*, motivated callers to work harder and ultimately have better outcomes. Thus, even within a prototypically meaningless job like telemarketing, the work can be "made" meaningful with demonstrable results. This study also highlights that, depending on how their work is designed, two people with the same role might view their work very differently in terms of its meaningfulness, and their satisfaction, commitment, and performance would differ as well. Importantly, as Grant's research demonstrates, the meaning people make of their work has the potential to be highly motivating; to translate into behavioral and economic outcomes that matter to individual employees and employers alike. This last point is consistent with psychologist Victor Frankl's observation that meaning is the "primary motivational force in man."

These findings raise several interesting observations regarding work meaning. First, they underscore the idea that something about the *work itself* matters for meaningfulness. When evaluating how meaningful versus meaningless a job is likely to be, it makes sense to evaluate, as Studs Terkel put it so eloquently in *Working*, "what [we] do all day, and how [we] feel about what we do." Looking at the basic elements of the tasks a job requires, like the amount of variety, repetition, autonomy, control, and recognition or feedback, gives insight into how meaningful the job will be. In addition, it appears that work can be essentially and easily manipulated to be more meaningful. Other studies confirm this effect. In one experimental setting, very mundane tasks, like spotting specific letters on a page, were made more significant when participant workers knew someone was going to review their work rather than either ignore it or shred it. In another, people were told that the images they were labeling were cancer tumors to aid medical researchers (versus not being told what the images were they were labeling), which increased their work output with no degradation in quality.

Second, these findings indicate that something about the *individual workers* also matters for work to be perceived as meaningful. One employee could view their work as pointless drudgery, whereas another, sitting right next to them, could see it as essential to another person's flourishing. As with much of social psychology, both individual disposition and elements of the social environment interact to produce any given employee's meaning of their work. This reinforces the claim we made earlier that work too has a subjective component.

One of the pioneers of contemporary psychological research on the meaning of work, Amy Wrzesniewski, who will feature prominently in this chapter, offers a third perspective on how people come to feel their work is meaningful: "the ways in which people *shape* their jobs to fit their unique orientation." This suggests a much more agentic role of employees in turning – to use a common expression – the jobs they have into the jobs they want. Writing with Jane Dutton, Wrzesniewski put forward a theory of *job crafting*, in which employees alter the task and/or relational boundaries of the work – that is, what they are doing or who they are doing it with and for – in order to make their work more meaningful.

One of the most poignant examples of job crafting used in this paper comes from hospital cleaners who, rather than having jobs described as "bullshit" are more emblematic of work deemed "essential" during the COVID-19 pandemic, and in earlier wartimes. Hospitals, like much of society, cannot function without sanitary work, but those workers rarely get the recognition or respect they deserve for their efforts that fall into a category sometimes referred to as "dirty work." Indeed, some of the hospital cleaners Wrzesniewski and Dutton interviewed – note that this was pre-pandemic – found their jobs to be both thankless and meaningless. The authors noted that this group of workers typically did not go out of their way to interact socially with others on the job, whether patients or other members of the hospital staff. Rather, this group performed the same cleaning tasks day after day, typically doing the bare minimum to be effective, almost as if checking off a list of rote tasks: dump the garbage cans, make the beds, etc. In other words, the cleaners in this category didn't assume much of their jobs and, in turn, their jobs didn't seem to provide them with much in the way of satisfaction or meaningfulness. Such workers stood in stark contrast to their colleagues who went out of their way to interact with others, whether patients – and the patients' families and friends – or their own co-workers at the hospital. This group consistently found ways to go above and beyond to do their jobs, whether attempting to clean in the most efficient way possible to match a patient's schedule or taking on additional tasks like directing visitors within the hospital. Importantly for the perspective of the meaning of their work, this group reframed the scope of their jobs from room cleaners to members of the patients' care team, along with physicians and nurses. The key idea behind job crafting is that, in just about any job or occupation, people with sufficient autonomy to do so can craft a more meaningful experience than they would otherwise have. This is not to say that, if people find themselves trapped in a meaningless job, they can simply job craft their way out of it. Nor is it to say that employers don't bear some responsibility for creating meaningful jobs. However, job crafting is meant to empower employees to at least try to make things better, even if only as a temporary lift as they search for new, more meaningful work.

These methods of job crafting – changing the task and relational boundaries, or said another way, what we do and whom we do it with or for – map very nicely onto two paths to creating meaningfulness at work identified by organizational psychologists Mike Pratt and Blake Ashforth. Pratt and Ashforth distinguish between what they term meaningfulness *in* work and meaningfulness *at* work. Meaningfulness *in work* addresses the question "What am I doing?" and speaks to one's role in an organization. For the hospital cleaners, this marks the difference between "room cleaner" and "member of the care team" and has implications for the types of work performed, from routine cleaning tasks to interacting with patients and their visitors and caregivers. Meaningfulness *at work* addresses the question "Where do I belong?" and speaks to one's membership in social groups. To return to the two groups of cleaners, one sees their work as a solitary pursuit, while the other sees it being part of a team. By specifying what one does and where one belongs, both meaningfulness in and at work have implications for individual work identity, which, in turn, leads to an overall sense of work as meaningful. Viewing meaning-making at work as being tied to individual identity, or the answer to the question "Who am I?", only serves to underscore that the process of making meaning is – at least in part – necessarily individual and subjective. This view is reinforced by one of the most popular ways we talk about the meaning of work to individuals: work orientation.

Work Orientations: Job, Career, and Calling

The book *Habits of the Heart* sought to answer the questions – as posed by the authors, sociologists Robert Bellah, Richard Madsen, William Sullivan,

Ann Swidler, and Steven Tipton in their 1996 updated edition – "How ought we to live? . . . Who are we, as Americans?" A deep, grounded investigation of, as the subtitle states, "Individualism and Commitment in American Life," *Habits of the Heart* clearly did not set out to be the ur-text for a future cadre of organizational psychologists interested in studying the meaning of work. The book mostly concerned itself with defining the spheres of public and private life to better understand, for example, how and why people weren't more engaged in civic life. In this way, it was an intellectual precursor to Richard Sennett's *The Corrosion of Character* and Robert Putnam's *Bowling Alone*, which tackled the same theme while more explicitly calling out the workplace as a driver of a decline in community. A mere five and a half pages of the 300+ pages that comprise *Habits of the Heart* are devoted to the section on "Work" – approximately the same amount as the preceding section on "Leaving Church." However, the length of this section belies the profundity of its insights – specifically, on the potential roles work plays in people's lives – which would, in turn, alter the way work meaning and meaningfulness would come to be studied in the decades that followed. Perhaps the outsized influence that the little section on work has had since the book's publication is a metaphor not only for how integral work is to all domains of American life but also to the life of any society.

The authors present "several different notions of work and of how it bears on who we are." According to their typology, people conceive of their work as a job, a career, or a calling. These terms all have pre-existing colloquial meanings, of course, but Bellah and colleagues use them here to denote the various meanings work can take on. When work is a *job*, it is primarily a means to make money in order to support life outside of work. Success here is defined by stability and financial reward. When work is a *career*, it is a means to ascend within a corporate or occupational hierarchy, as in an upward career ladder. Success in a career is marked by increasing power, status, and position. When work is a *calling*, by contrast, work is not a means to an end at all, but rather a meaningful end in itself. With a calling, success is less a focus than feeling part of a broader community and making a positive impact on others, whether specific beneficiaries – as in the college scholarship recipients mentioned earlier – or society as a whole. For those with the strongest callings, the authors write, "work constitutes a practical ideal of activity and character that makes a person's work morally inseparable from his or her life." This is an admittedly high bar: The authors follow four people throughout the book; yet, none of them is described as having a calling toward their work.

The book, though well-received and influential in its own right at the time of its publication, took on a new life when job, career, and calling were reintroduced by psychologists Amy Wrzesniewski, Clark McCauley, Paul Rozin, and Barry Schwartz as three *work orientations*, or ways people perceive their work. In their pioneering study, the authors asked people working in a variety of occupations and organizations to rate three paragraphs – each describing a person with a job, career, or calling orientation – in terms of how much each was like them. Respondents were clear and unambiguous in choosing one – and only one – description as most like them, and the distribution was roughly one-third for each, suggesting that no work orientation is more prominent than the others. Wrzesniewski and colleagues emphasized that job and career orientations were extrinsically motivated – that is, by factors external to the work like pay and promotions, respectively – whereas calling orientations were intrinsically motivated by the work itself. Work orientations matter for both individuals and organizations because they "determine our thoughts, feelings and behaviors toward work." In this regard, one of the most consistent findings in the initial 1997 paper was that callings appeared to be most beneficial across the board. Respondents reporting a calling orientation reported significantly higher satisfaction with both their jobs and their lives in general compared to the other two orientations, suggesting that callings not only benefit the proximal domain of work but life outside of work as well – although the distinction between work and life domains is admittedly blurred for those with strong callings. To wit, those with a calling orientation reported that they got more satisfaction from work than from hobbies or friends, while those with job and career orientations reported getting more satisfaction from the non-work domains. People with a calling orientation also reported higher income, level of education, social standing, and occupational status than those with the other two orientations, though what is cause and effect here is unclear, given the research methodology. Finally, those with calling orientations reported missing fewer days of work than those with job or career orientations. The authors then separately analyzed the single most common occupation in the data – administrative assistants (24 in total) – finding that, once again, they easily sorted into job (n = 9), career (n = 7), and calling (n = 8) orientations. Again, this reinforces that even within the same occupational role, and even within the same organization and job title, one person's job is another's career and yet another's calling.

Work as a Calling: It's Complicated

Although research on work orientation tends to emphasize all three orientations equally, research on the tripartite model has been eclipsed by a focus on one of the orientations: calling. There has been an unrelenting cultural *zeitgeist* emphasizing "Do what you love" (as in Steve Jobs' oft-quoted 2005 Stanford commencement speech) and "Find your calling" (as in recruiting website Monster.com's famous advertisement, "Your calling is calling"). This, coupled with and perhaps justified by the promising findings from Wrzesniewski and colleagues' initial study, has resulted in calling research exploding in the two-plus decades since. Callings seem to have both a practical and academic appeal, perhaps because they are "extreme cases" of people's devotion to their work, at once alluring, perhaps inexplicable, and useful for theory generation.

Of course, the notion of work as a calling is hardly new. Callings originated as an explicit calling from God toward ministerial work. The Protestant Reformation in the 15th–16th centuries broadened this definition. Martin Luther, founder of the Lutheran church, referred to calling as "any station that one might occupy in the world of productive work and suggested that through faithful execution of one's duties in that station, one both pleased God and contributed to the general welfare of humankind" (Luther, 1883). Bunderson and Thompson provide a detailed history of the religious origins and evolution of the notion of work as a calling in their influential paper on zookeepers, mentioned later. Apart from a few exceptions, like prostitution and usury, any occupation in Luther's view could be seen as equally worthy in God's eyes. This notion of calling connects to the Protestant Work Ethic – that hard work serves God and can be one's purpose in life. Work was thus elevated as a noble and moral pursuit, which stands in stark comparison to the Ancient Greek view that work served to distract people from finding their true purpose. As mentioned in a previous chapter, philosopher Joanne Ciulla describes work moving "from curse to calling." Theologian and founder of the Calvinist Christian doctrine, John Calvin believed not only that callings were based on our God-given gifts and talents but that following one's calling was a moral duty, on the order of a commandment from God. Centuries later, sociologist Max Weber would secularize calling and contend that it was used not only to ethically justify the division of labor in society but capitalism itself. According to this view, calling was effectively co-opted to justify the accumulation of not only occupational status but also wealth. Interestingly, over a century later, this critique of callings would re-emerge as a tool for employers to work employees harder and justify societal inequalities. Callings, it appears, perhaps because of their extreme nature, have always been complicated.

The paper that specifically studied calling in zookeepers presented it as a "painfully double-edged sword." This paper was based on a mixed method study, combining qualitative interviews to better understand the nature of the zookeepers' callings, and a quantitative survey to pinpoint the relationship between callings and important outcomes. Extending the notion from the initial paper by Wrzesniewski and colleagues that calling confers a host of benefits to employees and employers alike, the zookeeper paper revealed a more complicated story. On the one hand, much of what was revealed about calling so resembled the classical definition of calling in the Protestant Reformation view – that is, calling, for zookeepers, was a moral mandate, something they had felt compelled to do since they were little, propelled so strongly by their love of and concern for the welfare of animals that they literally couldn't imagine doing anything else – that the authors termed this view *neoclassical calling*. They defined a neoclassical calling as "that place in the occupational division of labor in society that one feels destined to fill by virtue of particular gifts, talents, and/or idiosyncratic life opportunities" (p. 38). There were benefits to this view: The zookeepers with strongest callings reported identifying more strongly with their occupations, which, in turn, made them feel their work was more meaningful and societally important. On the other hand, this strong sense of calling was both a blessing and a burden. Strong callings led the zookeepers to view the work as a moral duty, requiring them to go above and beyond at all times to care for the animals. Those with the strongest callings reported working more unpaid hours, overall lower income, and sacrifices of various kinds. One said:

> We don't get paid very well here. Actually, I work another job. I work seven days a week. I work two days at the art museum just to make ends meet. But I guess that's the payoff for doing what you love. I volunteered here for free for a year and a half.

One study identified a potential mechanism by which people with strong callings might be paid less: People reported feeling it is fair to pay those with strong passions for the work less than those without who are less passionate because the passion should be its own reward. The authors of the study termed this "legitimation of passion exploitation." Other studies have confirmed that those with stronger callings will put in more effort to perform tasks, even when they don't stand to gain additional money for their efforts. This raises a very real possibility, for those who are already in low-paying fields like zookeepers or artists, that they will experience real sacrifices to their quality and standard of living to perform the work they love.

Of course, one might reasonably ask why people would put up with such mistreatment; why they wouldn't recognize their right to fair wages and living standards. And it is possible they would, especially with external support from labor unions. However, Shasa Dobrow, an organizational behaviorist who studies callings among musicians – and has been a professional bassoonist herself – has termed the desire to pursue one's calling at any cost (financial or otherwise) a kind of career "tunnel vision." Musicians with strong callings were more likely to ignore the advice of a trusted mentor, in this case their music teachers, to not go into music, perhaps because they overestimated their own abilities relative to an objective assessment. Although, on average, musicians reported stronger callings, comparable to other artists, compared to managers or business students, the finding was replicated in a sample of business students with strong callings, who reported that they would be more likely to ignore a trusted mentor's advice to not pursue business compared to their lower-calling peers. For those of us who ever need to give career advice, it bears keeping in mind how callings have the ability to bias rational decision making about one's career options and preferences. But how much is too much when it comes to the tradeoffs one is willing to make to pursue a calling?

Researchers have distinguished between "healthy" and "unhealthy" pursuit of callings, where the latter can negatively affect relationships with one's co-workers. One of the zookeepers reported, "Working here at the zoo has cost me a marriage" (p. 42), indicating how calling can affect not only one's life at work but outside work as well. Of course, the opposite has been found to be true as well: A meta-analysis of calling studies spanning 20 years found that, when people experience their work as a calling, they experience overall hedonic and eudaimonic well-being. That is, calling contributes to an overall "good life," in addition to work meaningfulness and job satisfaction. Yet, it is difficult to avoid the conclusion that, perhaps at extreme levels, callings have the potential to tip in the direction of being a burden rather than a blessing.

What If We Are Mistaken about Meaning?

As we have seen, callings have the potential to alienate others, whether those with whom we work closely or those with whom we share a life. Up to this point, we have been treating the meaning that individuals make as purely determined by each individual for themself. Yet, of course, meaning making does not occur in a vacuum but is necessarily dependent on what we are do- ing and with whom we are doing it. Interacting with others at work has the potential to shape whether we view our work as a job, career, or calling, as our co-workers either reinforce or contradict the perceptions we have of our- selves. Similarly, romantic partners are vested stakeholders in how we view our work. One study by Winnie Jiang and Amy Wrzesniewski found that, when romantic partners experienced different work orientations – one views their job as a calling, the other as a career or job, for example – they reported greater uncertainty about the future and lower satisfaction for their jobs. This experience of what the authors called "work orientation incongruence" was so psychologically unsettling that, if one partner was unemployed, they were more likely to become reemployed over time compared to people whose partners' work orientations more closely matched their own.

What the study of romantic partners did not ask was how each partner viewed *the other's* work orientation and whether those views were congru- ent. We have reason to believe, however, that we do assess and judge the work orientations of people in our immediate surroundings, especially those with whom their work has the potential to provide for our lives – a spouse whose earnings allow the children to go to college debt-free, for example – or to take away from our lives – a spouse whose earnings allow great privileges at the cost of them being at the office almost all the time. Sometimes, our judgments are overly positive: One study found that managers who believed their subordinates had strong calling orientations believed them to be better performers and more committed to the organization, even when there was no evidence to support this perception. Sometimes, our judgments are overly negative: Another study revealed that co-workers with strong intrinsic moti- vation for the job (as in a calling) viewed those who were not as motivated negatively, believed they were less moral, and offered them less help as a result. These findings indicate that we have the potential to be wrong about both the work meaning of others as well as what it means.

Part of our judgment about the work orientations of others, whether significant others, parents, children, or co-workers, might be whether the value they get from their work is worth the price they pay to perform that work. Of course, that judgment also might have something to do with cultural views dictating what work is worth doing and what sacrifices are worth making. Military spouses, for example, often spend long periods of deployment as single parents understanding the tradeoff for their spouse's careers and the broader goal of national security. It is likely not a coincidence that both studies we cited previously confirm the view of calling as being somehow superior to, more desirable than, and even more moral than that of a job or career. Using a distinction we have already introduced, we can say that work orientation is a *descriptive* construct – helping us to understand *how people behave* – whereas meaning and purpose also have a *prescriptive* (or *normative*, as philosophers more often say) dimension worth exploring – about how people *ought to be*.

Studies about normative work orientation are few. We have advocated, in our own research and writing, for scholars to consider meaning and purpose not just from the first-person perspective of the worker but also from the third-person perspective of others who are affected by the work. In one paper, we used Studs Terkel's *Working* as well as the Portraits of Grief as examples of what we can learn when we consider others' perspectives. In both cases, what is revealed is more complex than what we learn from first-person reflections, in part because these outside perspectives hold up a societal mirror to present what they value most about the person's work. When we think about why we ourselves work, we might think about what we get from work in a narrow way: money, status, or meaningfulness. When we think about why others work, we think about impact in a much broader way. Our analysis of the portraits really brings this point home, where ultimate impact points to both a broadening and a finality. Of course, these memorials cannot reveal the actual meanings the deceased would have ascribed to their work; however, they attest to the lasting legacy of this work on those left behind.

One of the most surprising things we found when we analyzed and coded the Portraits of Grief, following the established research method for content analysis, was that the vast majority – about two-thirds – did not give enough information about the victims' work to clearly code for a job, career, or calling. In these portraits, which we concluded portrayed work as incidental to the subject's life as a whole, little more was given than the person's occupation, job title, and/or employer. As noted previously, though, in other studies of work orientation, job, career, and calling orientations are roughly evenly distributed, in our study, callings were slightly more than one-third, and jobs, slightly less. Needless to say, the portraits in which someone seemed to view the work that brought them to the site of the attacks on 9/11 as a job usually offered an alternative endeavor that was closer to a calling, as in the portrait of bond trader Glen Thompson, whose wife reflected, "He was a bond trader and damn good at it. But his heart and soul were outdoors." Mr. Thompson apparently wished to retire early and move to Colorado to enjoy the outdoors full-time.

Another surprising thing we found was that the view of job orientations as being the lowest and least desirable form of work orientation, stereotypically described as "just a job," was far more complicated and contested in the portraits. For example, in the traditional presentation of work orientation through workers' own eyes, calling is the only work orientation that allows for societal impact: Work is fulfilling, in part, because it makes the world a better place or serves moral aims. Yet, in the portraits, we see evidence of the lowly job orientation being elevated to a noble end, as in the portrait of Mohammed Chowdhury:

> He was supporting his pregnant wife and 6-year-old daughter by serving banquets at Windows on the World, but that was only temporary. He had a master's degree in physics from Bangladesh, where he grew up, and had studied real estate and computer science in this country. After a few doleful years in Baltimore, he was determined to stay in New York. He knew something good would come up.

Mr. Chowdhury's long-awaited baby boy would be born on September 13. Although his work as a server could be described as a job – or, more generously, as a career, a stepping stone to something better – it served to provide for his growing family. The portrait of Hector Tirado, Jr. expressed a similar sentiment in more colorful terms. A firefighter, waiter, and occasional model, Mr. Tirado's uncle remembered him saying about his modeling work, "As long as it's legitimate and I make money for my children, I don't care." Mr. Tirado had five children under the age of 11 to support.

Similarly, although career orientations are typically presented as being about little besides the worker's own career ascension and progress, extrinsically motivated, and self-benefiting, we did see evidence of careers that served societally beneficial ends. Typically, these were inspirational, where the career-holder served as a role model – proof that one's hard work and upward mobility could overcome challenges. For example, Pamela Chu was a Korean immigrant who worked her way up to being an equities trader at Cantor Fitzgerald. Ms. Chu's close friend recalled, "She was the only female trader and only Asian in her department, and that was difficult, but she seemed so relaxed." Richard A. Penny spent ten years without a permanent home; however, the former high school valedictorian worked to gain a steady job with a recycling program that allowed him to rent a room. His case worker remembers: "He totally went against all the stereotypes of homeless folks," describing him as soft-spoken, hard-working, with a penchant for learning.

Finally, even the view of callings presented in the portraits was complex and nuanced. As mentioned in an earlier chapter, work can be meaningful because of self-realization or service to others. Similarly, callings have been found to be both inwardly and outwardly focused. In one study, we compared the portraits of financiers and first responders – the two largest occupational groups among 9/11 victims – who were remembered as having calling orientations toward their work. We expected to find more self-focused stories among financiers and more other-focused stories among first responders. The former proved to be true. For most financiers, their callings were expressed as the pure love of the work itself, for the challenge, long hours, and/or competition, as in a self-focused calling. For example, Atsushi Shiratori was described as being "passionate about his job, and so obsessed with the stock market that he once spent a two-week vacation in a day-trading salon, buying and selling stocks." But a few financiers were cited as having a calling that was other-focused. Charles A. Zion, Executive Vice President at Cantor, was one such person, having taken up golf to have a second love after his job. His son laments, "I was looking forward to having him mentor me. He really loved teaching people the market," speaking to Mr. Zion's desire to share his passion with others, helping them to do the job that brought him so much joy.

A starker contrast still was to first responders, many of whom were remembered as having other-oriented callings – a finding that might seem unsurprising and even prototypical, given the nature of the work. Port Authority Police Officer Greg Froehner was described as "yearn[ing] for a job where he could serve others" since he was a boy. Firefighter Kevin Smith's sister said, "He just had this desire to serve." All of Mr. Smith's children entered service professions, including his son, an FDNY emergency medical officer, who was also at the Twin Towers on 9/11 and survived. Similar to the other-oriented career orientations, some first responders were role models, such as Keithroy Maynard, who joined a group of black firefighters who tried to increase diversity in the force. His twin brother remembered, "People do look to you. You're like a role model in a sense, especially in the black community where there aren't many black firefighters."

So, whose meaning matters more: our own sense of what our work is for or the perception of those around us? The former might explain our own motivation: why we show up each day, put in our all, help others, make sacrifices – or do none of these things! In turn, this effort has its own societal impact and personal (if not always professional) reward. The latter, however, reveals the ultimate impact of our work in terms of how those closest to us experience it. Whether that work is seen as a job, career, or calling, in the eyes of others, our work can serve our own self-realization, but it can also serve to help others, including those doing the reflecting who valued what we did. Children learn from their parents' examples how to approach their work in terms of meaning. Spouses build a life together that may be congruent or incongruent in terms of meaning. And in the very final analysis, when we all leave behind our work – and our lives – our legacy, in part, is in the eyes of those who remain who knew us best and work to share or emulate these legacies.

Questions and Prompts for Review and Reflection About Chapter 3

- What is the most Sisyphean (meaningless) work you can imagine? What makes it meaningless? In the spirit of job crafting, what changes can you imagine making to the work to make the experience of performing it more meaningful?
- In your own words, define jobs, careers, and callings. What are the key differences between them?
- Which would you prefer to have: a job, career, or calling? Give an example of a type of work that for you would constitute:

  - A job?
  - A career?
  - A calling?

- Reflect on your own work or that of someone you have interviewed for your reflections in prior chapters. How might its meaningfulness (or meaninglessness) in the eyes of others be consistent with – or different from – its meaningfulness in the eyes of the worker themself?
- Consider your foregoing examples of work that, for you, would constitute a job, career, or calling. How is that job, career, or calling self-serving? In what ways might it serve others – or, if it does not, how might it be crafted in such a way as to serve others?

Chapter 3 References

Amabile, Teresa M., Karl G. Hill, Beth A. Hennessey, and Elizabeth M. Tighe. "The Work Preference Inventory: Assessing Intrinsic and Extrinsic Motivational Orientations." *Journal of Personality and Social Psychology* 66, no. 5 (1994): 950–967. https://doi.org/10.1037/0022-3514.66.5.950

Ariely, Dan, Emir Kamenica, and Dražen Prelec. "Man's Search for Meaning: The Case of Legos." *Journal of Economic Behavior & Organization* 67, no. 3–4 (2008): 671–677. https://doi.org/10.1016/j.jebo.2008.01.004

Ashforth, Blake E., and Glen E. Kreiner. "'How Can You Do It?': Dirty Work and the Challenge of Constructing a Positive Identity." *Academy of Management Review* 24, no. 3 (1999): 413–434. https://doi.org/10.5465/amr.1999.2202129

Bellah, Robert N., Richard Madsen, William M. Sullivan, Ann Swidler, and Steven M. Tipton. *Habits of the Heart: Individualism and Commitment in American Life.* New York: Harper & Row, 1985.

Bunderson, J. Stuart, and Jeffrey A. Thompson. "The Call of the Wild: Zookeepers, Callings, and the Double-Edged Sword of Deeply Meaningful Work." *Administrative Science Quarterly* 54, no. 1 (2009): 32–57. https://doi.org/10.2189/asqu.2009.54.1.32

Calvin, John. *Sermons of M. John Calvin Upon the Epistle of Saint Paul to the Galatians.* London: Lucas Harison and George Bishop, 1574.

Cardador, M. Teresa, and Brianna B. Caza. "Relational and Identity Perspectives on Healthy Versus Unhealthy Pursuit of Callings." *Journal of Career Assessment* 20, no. 3 (2012): 338–353. https://doi.org/10.1177/1069072711436162

Cech, Erin A. *The Trouble with Passion: How Searching for Fulfillment at Work Fosters Inequality.* Berkeley, CA: University of California Press, 2021.

Chandler, Dana, and Adam Kapelner. "Breaking Monotony with Meaning: Motivation in Crowdsourcing Markets." *Journal of Economic Behavior & Organization* 90 (2013): 123–133. https://doi.org/10.1016/j.jebo.2013.03.003

Cho, Yuna, and Winnie Y. Jiang. "How Work Orientation Impacts Objective Career Outcomes via Managerial (Mis)perceptions." *Academy of Management Journal* 65, no. 4 (2022): 1353–1382. https://doi.org/10.5465/amj.2020.0841

Ciulla, Joanne B. *The Working Life: The Promise and Betrayal of Modern Work.* New York: Currency, 2001.

Dekas, Kathryn H., and Wayne E. Baker. "Adolescent Socialization and the Development of Adult Work Orientations." In *Adolescent Experiences and Adult Work Outcomes: Connections and Causes* (Research in the Sociology of Work, vol. 25), 51–84. Emerald Group Publishing Limited, 2014. https://doi.org/10.1108/S0277-283320140000025003

Dobrow, Shoshana R. "Extreme Subjective Career Success: A New Integrated View of Having a Calling." In *Academy of Management Proceedings*, vol. 2004, no. 1, B1–B6. Briarcliff Manor, NY: Academy of Management, 2004.

Dobrow, Shoshana R., and Daniel Heller. "Follow Your Heart or Your Head? A Longitudinal Study of the Facilitating Role of Calling and Ability in the Pursuit of a Challenging Career." *Journal of Applied Psychology* 100, no. 3 (2015): 695–712. https://doi.org/10.1037/a0038011

Dobrow, Shoshana R., and Jennifer Tosti-Kharas. "Calling: The Development of a Scale Measure." *Personnel Psychology* 64, no. 4 (2011): 1001–1049. https://doi.org/10.1111/j.1744-6570.2011.01234.x

Dobrow, Shoshana R., and Jennifer Tosti-Kharas. "Listen to Your Heart? Calling and Receptivity to Career Advice." *Journal of Career Assessment* 20, no. 3 (2012): 264–280. https://doi.org/10.1177/1069072711434412

Dobrow, Shoshana R., Hannah Weisman, Daniel Heller, and Jennifer Tosti-Kharas. "Calling and the Good Life: A Meta-Analysis and Theoretical Extension." *Administrative Science Quarterly* 68, no. 2 (2023): 508–550. https://doi.org/10.1177/00018392231159641

Eisenhardt, Kathleen M. "Building Theories from Case Study Research." *Academy of Management Review* 14, no. 4 (1989): 532–550. https://doi.org/10.5465/amr.1989.4308385

Fox, Killian. "Boots Riley: 'In Film, the More Personal You Get, the More Universal You Get'." *The Guardian.* November 25, 2018. www.theguardian.com/film/2018/nov/25/boots-riley-musician-director-sorry-to-bother-you-interview

Frankl, Viktor E. *Man's Search for Meaning.* New York: Pocket Books, 1985.

Furnham, Adrian. "The Protestant Work Ethic: A Review of the Psychological Literature." *European Journal of Social Psychology* 14, no. 1 (1984): 87–104. https://doi.org/10.1002/ejsp.2420140108

Graeber, David. *Bullshit Jobs: A Theory.* New York: Simon & Schuster, 2018.

Grant, Adam M., Elizabeth M. Campbell, Grace Chen, Keenan Cottone, David Lapedis, and Karen Lee. "Impact and the Art of Motivation Maintenance: The Effects of Contact with Beneficiaries on Persistence Behavior." *Organizational Behavior and Human Decision Processes* 103, no. 1 (2007): 53–67. https://doi.org/10.1016/j.obhdp.2006.05.004

Graves, Donna. "What WWII Can Teach Us about Essential Work." *The Hill.* April 26, 2020. https://thehill.com/blogs/congress-blog/politics/494690-if-this-is-our-world-war-two-moment/

Gross, Terry. "Boots Riley Mines His Experiences as a Telemarketer in 'Sorry to Bother You'." *Fresh Air.* July 2, 2018. www.npr.org/2018/07/02/625321886/boots-riley-mines-his-experiences-as-a-telemarketer-in-sorry-to-bother-you

Guevara, Karmen, and Jacqueline Ord. "The Search for Meaning in a Changing Work Context." *Futures* 28, no. 8 (1996): 709–722. https://doi.org/10.1016/0016-3287(96)00030-4

Hackman, J. Richard, and Greg R. Oldham. "Motivation Through the Design of Work: Test of a Theory." *Organizational Behavior and Human Performance* 16, no. 2 (1976): 250–279. https://doi.org/10.1016/0030-5073(76)90016-7

Jaffe, Sarah. *Work Won't Love You Back: How Devotion to Our Jobs Keeps Us Exploited, Exhausted, and Alone.* New York: Bold Type Books, 2021.

Jiang, Winnie Y., and Amy Wrzesniewski. "Misaligned Meaning: Couples' Work-Orientation Incongruence and Their Work Outcomes." *Organization Science* 33, no. 2 (2022): 785–809. https://doi.org/10.1287/orsc.2021.1453

Jobs, Steve. "You've Got to Find What You Love." Transcript of Speech Delivered at Stanford University. June 12, 2005. https://news.stanford.edu/2005/06/12/youve-got-find-love-jobs-says/

Kim, Jae Yun, Troy H. Campbell, Steven Shepherd, and Aaron C. Kay. "Understanding Contemporary Forms of Exploitation: Attributions of Passion Serve to Legitimize the Poor Treatment of Workers." *Journal of Personality and Social Psychology* 118, no. 1 (2020): 121–148. https://doi.org/10.1037/pspi0000190

Kwon, Mijeong, Julia Lee Cunningham, and Jon M. Jachimowicz. "Discerning Saints: Moralization of Intrinsic Motivation and Selective Prosociality at Work." *Academy of Management Journal* 66, no. 6 (2023): 1625–1650. https://doi.org/10.5465/amj.2020.1761

Luther, Martin. *Werke: Kritische Gesamtausgabe.* Weimar: Hermann Böhlaus, 1910.

Michaelson, Christopher, and Jennifer Tosti-Kharas. "Serving Self or Serving Others? Close Relations' Perspectives on Ethics and Calling." *Journal of Vocational Behavior* 114 (2019): 19–30. https://doi.org/10.1016/j.jvb.2019.02.005

Monster.com. "Your Calling Is Calling." *Video from YouTube.* Accessed February 26, 2024. www.youtube.com/watch?v=Xam7Dws_UfU

Pratt, Michael G., and Blake E. Ashforth. "Fostering Meaningfulness in Working and at Work." In *Positive Organizational Scholarship: Foundations of a New Discipline,* edited by Kim S. Cameron, Jane E. Dutton, and Robert E. Quinn, 309–327. Oakland, CA: Berrett-Koehler, 2003.

Putnam, Robert D. *Bowling Alone: The Collapse and Revival of American Community*. New York: Touchstone Books by Simon & Schuster, 2001.

Schabram, K., and S. Maitlis. "Negotiating the Challenges of a Calling: Emotion and Enacted Sensemaking in Animal Shelter Work." *Academy of Management Journal* 60, no. 2 (2017): 584–609. https://doi.org/10.5465/amj.2013.0665

Schwartz, Adina. "Meaningful Work." *Ethics* 92, no. 4 (1982): 634–646. www.jstor.org/stable/2380395

Sennett, Richard. *The Corrosion of Character: The Personal Consequences of Work in the New Capitalism*. New York: W.W. Norton, 2000.

Terkel, Studs. *Working: What People Do All Day and How They Feel About What They Do*. New York: Pantheon Books, 1974.

Thompson, Jeffery A., and J. Stuart Bunderson. "Research on Work as a Calling . . . and How to Make It Matter." *Annual Review of Organizational Psychology and Organizational Behavior* 6 (2019): 421–443. https://doi.org/10.1146/annurev-orgpsych-012218-015140

Tosti-Kharas, Jennifer, Shoshana R. Dobrow, and Heather Barry Kappes. "Do What You Love and You'll Never Work a Day in Your Life? Testing Fundamental Assumptions about Calling, Effort, and Enjoyment." *Journal of Management Scientific Reports*. In press.

Tosti-Kharas, Jennifer, and Christopher Michaelson. "To Mean Is to Be Perceived: Studying the Meaning of Work Through the Eyes of Others." *Academy of Management Perspectives* 35, no. 3 (2021): 503–516. https://doi.org/10.5465/amp.2018.0156

Weber, Max. *The Protestant Ethic and the Spirit of Capitalism*. New York: Dover, 2003.

Weber, Robert. *Basic Content Analysis*. Thousand Oaks, CA: Sage, 1990.

Wrzesniewski, Amy. "Finding Positive Meaning in Work." In *Positive Organizational Scholarship: Foundations of a New Discipline*, edited by Kim S. Cameron, Jane E. Dutton, and Robert E. Quinn, 296–308. Oakland, CA: Berrett-Koehler, 2003.

Wrzesniewski, Amy, and Jane E. Dutton. "Crafting a Job: Revisioning Employees as Active Crafters of Their Work." *Academy of Management Review* 26, no. 2 (2001): 179–201. https://doi.org/10.5465/amr.2001.4378011

Wrzesniewski, Amy, Jane E. Dutton, and Gelaye Debebe. "Interpersonal Sensemaking and the Meaning of Work." *Research in Organizational Behavior* 25 (2003): 93–135. https://doi.org/10.1016/S0191 3085(03)25003-6

Wrzesniewski, Amy, Clark McCauley, Paul Rozin, and Barry Schwartz. "Jobs, Careers, and Callings: People's Relations to Their Work." *Journal of Research in Personality* 31, no. 1 (1997): 21–33. https://doi.org/10.1006/jrpe.1997.2162

4   A Framework of Frameworks of What Work Is For

Are There More Than Three Reasons People Work?

You may have wondered to yourself as you were reading about jobs, careers, and callings whether there are any other reasons to work that they do not capture. As we have seen from examples earlier in the book, some people work for companionship, and others, to alleviate boredom. Are those jobs, careers, callings, or none of the above? In *Shop Class as Soulcraft*, Matthew Crawford – a political scientist who owned a motorcycle repair shop – reported on the satisfaction he experienced tinkering with engines, which speaks to applying one's manual skills to solve a problem. He made money doing it, but he likely could have made more doing something else that utilized his doctorate. As a sole proprietor, he was not seeking to climb any organizational hierarchy. And though he enjoyed working on motorcycles, he may not have written a book about it if his one true calling had been just to fix them. That there are experiences of work that do not neatly fit into the job, career, and calling categories raises the question: Are there other work orientations out there?

For that matter, are work orientations literally "out there" in the world, or are they, rather, states of mind that are "in us" – the worker or others who perceive the work? Philosophical idealists like George Berkeley are inclined to answer that our entire experience of the world is a matter of perception over reality, or in other words, to contend that perception *is* reality. Although we might take issue with that relatively extreme conclusion, we do believe that linguistic philosophers are right to observe that the relationship between the words we use and the world we live in is a two-way street. Ludwig Wittgenstein observes that, when we are young, we learn language by pointing to objects to which a word name has been assigned. As our understanding of language matures, however, we can see how the language we use influences our experience of the world. For example, if we are told that there are three ways in which people relate to their work, we might be inclined to accept that there are *only* three work orientations, and if we always hear them referred to as jobs first, careers second, and callings third, we might come to the conclusion that jobs are the most basic and callings are the most important.

DOI: 10.4324/9781003307327-4

Yet, if our experience challenges that classification and/or that hierarchy, we might need to expand our lexicon to match the world we live in.

All of which is to say that we believe that work orientations have explanatory value that can help us make sense of our experience of the world of work. However, we do not think – nor do we believe the originators of work orientation theory intended – that they could exhaustively capture the ways in which we might relate to our work, nor how we *ought to* relate to our work. Kira Schabram, Jordan Nielsen, and Jeffrey Thompson recently added a fourth work orientation to the job-career-calling construct, which they characterize as a kind of combination of career and calling, in which the worker wants to "be or do more" – or both. In another challenge to the conventional work orientation framework, Laura Boova, Mike Pratt, and Doug Lepisto proposed six alternative work orientations to explain "what made work worth doing." Four of them map fairly neatly to job ("utilitarian"), career ("status"), and calling ("passion" and "service"), but two of them ("craftsmanship" and "kinship") imply other relationships to work that, as we have suggested previously, may not be captured by the original work orientations alone.

These attempts to muddy the waters of work orientation are both evidence of the extraordinary explanatory power of job-career-calling and the extraordinary complexity of explaining why we work. There may well be infinite work orientations, depending upon how you look at the problem phenomenologically. However, we have noticed that many other attempts to account for why we work, how we feel about it, and – perhaps most important – what reasons we ought to (and ought not to) work for consist, coincidentally or not, of three elements. This raises another question: Are there fundamentally three types of work, or do our minds conveniently classify phenomena into three categories? We think it is more likely that our minds like to work in threes, but what is even more interesting to us is that there is substantial overlap among several of these tripartite classification systems. These additional constructs come from a variety of sources: social science, of course, but also philosophy, political science, our own classrooms, and even the musings of workers themselves. In the remainder of this chapter, we endeavor to explore these theories of work and to consider their further explanatory value in making sense of anyone's experience of work – by testing them on two very different characters at different junctures in their working lives.

Fatou and Fogle are both fictional characters, but one of the reasons it makes sense to study them in order to understand how real people relate to work is that fiction provides us greater access into the minds of other people than reality ever offers. Through fiction, we can literally get inside the thoughts of characters about their hopes, dreams, and regrets, whereas we can only infer the reasons and motivations of real people from what they say and do. The ancient Greek philosopher Aristotle contended that the lessons of fiction are more universal than those of reality because fiction engages the human imagination to speculate about myriad possibilities, whereas history only tells us about the one that actually transpired. In that vein, researchers in recent decades have shown that fiction has the potential to cultivate a variety of desirable social traits, including empathy, ability to relate to other people, and emotional intelligence, among others. These traits, in turn, are among the moral virtues that enable us to experience meaning and purpose and to cultivate them in the lives of others.

Fatou is the central character in Zadie Smith's short story, "The Embassy of Cambodia," a tale about the experience of a maid working for a wealthy family in London. Their home happens to be near the embassy of Cambodia, where the shuttlecock that is smashed back and forth in a seemingly endless game of badminton seems to be a metaphor for Fatou's absence of freedom. Chris Fogle is the first-person narrator of Chapter 22 of *The Pale King*, David Foster Wallace's posthumously published novel about boredom at work set at the United States Internal Revenue Service. The chapter has also been republished as a stand-alone novella under the title *Something to Do with Paying Attention*, a phrase that captures Fogle's discovery of tax accounting but also of himself. Though Smith was 13 years younger, she and Wallace were contemporaries and friends, hailed as two of the most gifted and exciting authors of their generation, who first broke on the scene at the turn of the century with the big and inscrutable novels *White Teeth* and *Infinite Jest* and followed upon those triumphs with more critically acclaimed books. She once joked about him admiringly, "Wallace is proving to be the kind of writer I was sort of hoping didn't exist – a visionary, a craftsman, a comedian . . . [who] can do anything with a piece of prose. . . . Goddamn him." Although Wallace left behind a complicated legacy after his untimely death in 2008, at a memorial service in his honor, Smith ironically compared his story collection *Brief Interviews with Hideous Men* – narratives of men who are misogynistic, violent, and perverted – to "being in church."

By contrast, Fatou's and Fogle's stories are about being at work, which is sometimes hideous but possibly enlightening. Both characters are in the first decade of adulthood, but their experiences of work are significantly different. Fatou is a woman of color; Fogle is a White man. She is African; he is American; she works in the United Kingdom; he studies in the United States; she is a manual laborer; he is a knowledge worker; she is religious; he is a nihilist; she works hard in a vain struggle to escape material poverty; and he is born into middle class comfort that seems to drain him of any sense of industry. Despite these differences, they also seem to share in the universal search for meaning and purpose at work and in life.

Job, Career, Calling (Reprise)

In the language of work orientations, Fatou's story is that of a job orientation in search of a career without the wherewithal to dream of a calling. Her father had taken her from the Ivory Coast to Ghana at age 16, where they both worked at a hotel. After a guest apparently rapes her, her father spends much of his savings to secure her passage from Accra to Libya to Italy. She ends up in London working for the Derawals – a family with three children that owns and operates several convenience stores. Fatou cooks and cleans and even cares for the children, forging something of a career that she hopes may lead to something better someday, whereas, as a hotel maid, she would have been stuck in the same place doing the same things forever. However, the Derawals keep Fatou's passport and pay her only in room and board, meaning she has neither the money nor the papers to find another employer. The only freedom she experiences is when the parents are working, the kids are at school, and she steals one of their guest passes to swim at the pool at the health center down the street. On her walk, she passes the embassy of Cambodia, where the endless *pock-smash* of the shuttlecock seems like a metaphor for Fatou's condition, swatted back and forth by external forces more powerful than she is.

Fogle also languishes in a series of jobs, even though he has the parental and economic support to get a college degree. He leaves school three times due to lack of motivation and lands in "so-called real jobs," including "the production line at a Cheese Nabs plant working the cheese product injector." Finding such positions "unbelievably boring and meaningless" leads him back to school, but, as he bounces from job to job and college to college with little sense of inner direction, his father despairs about his son's lack of career ambition. In college, Fogle does a lot of drugs and watches too much television. Only after his father dies in what Christopher has written about as "arguably one of the most spectacularly descriptive tragicomic scenes in the entire history of literature" does Fogle literally stumble upon his calling by entering the wrong classroom. Ironically and also perhaps comically, in that classroom, he becomes enthralled with tax accounting, a profession that Wallace chose for his novel as the archetype of boring work. In other chapters of *The Pale King*, one character dies slumped over his desk but nobody notices, and another contemplates suicide waiting for his next break.

Labor, Work, Action

Fatou's first job as a hotel maid was what we colloquially refer to as *labor* – manual activity demanding physical exertion. However, philosopher and historian Hannah Arendt's conception of *labor* as the lowest form of the *vita activa* – active life – may be as much about mental as physical exertion. If you have never worked as a maid yourself but you have been the beneficiary of their labor, try to imagine the experience from their perspective. Smith's story does not detail Fatou's work as a maid, perhaps because it is too dull to recount, though we will try, nonetheless, to do so here. She may never have seen the hotel guests whose messes she cleaned up; she probably did not regularly receive expressions of gratitude; her performance may have been measured by the speed with which she performed her perfunctory tasks of wiping the counters, vacuuming the rugs, cleaning the toilets, and so on, affording her no opportunity to luxuriate on the beds she unmade and remade; and, when she completed the assignment of tidying up one room, she probably went on to the next one to start all over again. Labor, in Arendt's framework that is set out in her book *The Human Condition*, is a struggle for survival, rather than satisfaction, and money, rather than meaning. In that sense, it shares some characteristics of the job in Wrzesniewski's framework except that Wrzesniewski's job-holder theoretically may consider her job as a means to better ends outside of work, as we saw in some Portraits of Grief, whereas Arendt's laborer may have no way out of the repetitive cycle of her condition. Ironically, only the appearance of "the Devil," as Fatou thinks of the hotel guest who forced himself upon her, leads to her departure from her deleterious existence as a hotel maid.

The next level of Arendt's *vita activa* is *work*, which may also involve mental and physical exertion but does so to the end of producing a permanent object. Whereas Fatou's labor as a maid is constantly done only to be undone, the prospect of work opens up the possibility that what she produces might have staying power. Whether this possibility is a reality in her experience as the Derawals' maid is a matter for debate, however. She keeps house for the Derawals much as she did for her hotel guests, cleaning and folding their laundry only for it to get unfolded and soiled again. She cooks food for it to be consumed. She even saves the life of one of their children who is choking, only to be reprimanded by Mrs. Derawal for not minding her own business. Often, the children call her stupid and insult her skin color, and she is sometimes slapped by her bosses. One day, after reading a newspaper story about a slave who is kept prisoner in a rich man's house in London, she asks herself whether she is a slave. Even though, without any money or her passport, she has no means of escape from her position, she concludes that she is not a slave because she is free to shop for the Derawals' groceries and would have evenings to socialize if she had the funds to do so. However, it remains unclear whether her labor rises to the level of work that will lead anywhere.

Only after she is dismissed from the Derawals' employment does Fatou rise to the level of *action*, the highest level of Arendt's *vita activa*. Action, according to Arendt, reveals the self that individuates one person from others. At the end of the story, as she is packing her bags, Fatou asks for her passport which Mrs. Derawals denies any knowledge of, only later to slip it under the door. Fatou calls her only friend in London who says he will try to find her a position at his workplace cleaning the offices. Of course, if she accepts the offer, she will be a maid all over again, but this time, she can hope, she will have an independent income and be free from abuse. Though she has no clear plan for where her passport will take her, Fatou has regained a measure of control over her own life or action.

Labor, Workmanship, Calling

As we have noted before, work orientations are *descriptive* accounts about how people actually relate to their work, whereas Arendt's *vita activa* is a *prescriptive* account in which *action* is better than *work* and *work* is better than *labor*. Philosopher Gregory Pence's framework of labor, workmanship, and calling is also prescriptive and begins with *labor* as less desirable and ends with *calling*, which he characterizes as more desirable. This prioritization, again, stands in contrast to Wrzesniewski's job, career, calling version, which does not explicitly privilege one classification over another, no matter their implicit societal hierarchy.

Pence says in his essay "Towards a Theory of Work," that one feature of labor that is undesirable is that it is "very unpleasant for the worker" because it is: "(1) repetitious, (2) not intrinsically satisfying, (3) done out of necessity . . . [and] involves (4) few higher human faculties, and (5) little choice about how and when the work is done." Fogle includes not only the Cheese Nabs plant but also working as a security guard in a parking garage, taking tickets at a sports arena, and manufacturing and installing gymnasium floors among his laborious pursuits that were so devoid of satisfaction that they led him back to school for which he also had little enthusiasm.

Perhaps Fogle's discovery of *workmanship*, the next higher classification in Pence's framework, is in the same classroom where he discovers his calling. On his way to a review session for a political science final exam in 311 Daniel Hall, he inexplicably takes a wrong turn and ends up in 311 Garnier Hall – an identical-looking space where an Advanced Tax class is taking place. Too embarrassed to cause a commotion by getting up and leaving, Fogle begins to observe the students around him, some of whom turn out to be graduate students preparing for their chosen profession. To this point, Fogle had expressed no interest in accounting except to barely pass an Introduction to Accounting class that he took to please his father, who was usually displeased with him. The climactic scene of his father's disappointment with Fogle is when the older man returns home earlier than expected from a professional conference wearing a suit and chapeau, only to discover the younger man with his friends in a disheveled state doing bong hits in a catastrophically messy living room. Fogle and his father never speak about the incident, which symbolizes how neat and orderly – and boring – the older man's life is, in comparison to his son's life. Back in the Advanced Tax classroom, Fogle observes students wearing suits and carrying "actual briefcases and accordion files instead of backpacks" and "suddenly felt uncomfortable about my painter's pants and untied Timberlands." He also notices that some of them "had multiple pencils lined up on their desks, all of which were extremely sharp" and hears their watch alarms ring at the same time when the hour is up. Of course, these perceptions are just superficial signs of the accountant's *workmanship*, which Pence characterizes as pertaining both to "professional occupations like dentistry and engineering" as well as manual but precision work "like carpentry, leather-working, etc." *Workmanship*, according to Pence, involves: "(1) use of higher human faculties, (2) some intrinsic satisfaction in the activity itself, (3) some degree of choice about when work is done and how, (4) pride of the worker in the products of his work."

In Wallace's caricature of the accountant, their dress and mannerisms are as precise as the matching numbers at the bottom of the balance sheet.

Throughout his narrative, Fogle displays a peculiar tic of counting words: the total words in his entire story, the number of words uttered in a lecture by a professor, and even how many words it takes his father to upbraid him. This, no doubt, is a sign that a profession involving counting things might turn out to be a perfect fit for Fogle. Pence says that a *calling* is "the highest kind of activity involving work" and enables: "(1) development and exercise of unique personal qualities, (2) intrinsic satisfaction in the activity, (3) personal choice in accepting the job in the first place" – in other words, not so different from a calling orientation, absent the evaluative judgment. But what really inspires Fogle to discover his calling in tax accounting are the inspirational concluding words of the lecturer in the class he accidentally enters. He intones: "I wish to inform you that the accounting profession to which you aspire is, in fact, heroic." For anyone who has ever referred to accountants as "bean counters," the association of this seemingly dull and monotonous profession with such other words as "romantic" and "chivalric" seems ironic if not parody. But the lecturer goes on to say that the heroism of accounting consists in giving order to the world's chaos, even if doing so is stereotypically dull: "Enduring tedium over time in a confined space is what real courage is." As the session nears a conclusion for which the lecturer will receive not applause but rather a collective "ecstatic spasm," Fogle realizes that he has been so mesmerized by the speech that he has lost count: "It suddenly occurred to me that I had no idea how many words he'd spoken since that 8,206th one at the conclusion of the review." Interestingly, the person who professes these words happens to be a Jesuit priest. Fogle compares the moment of discovering his calling to the very type of religious experience that not long before he had been making fun of when his roommate's girlfriend claims to be a born-again Christian.

Market Fit, Self-Realization, Service to Others

All the frameworks to this point primarily consider our reasons to work as subjective in origin. That is to say that we work for *our own* reasons, not because others *decide for us*. To a certain extent, that makes sense and is consistent with prior findings from psychology that people were distributed across work orientations, even when they all basically did the same type of work. Similarly, philosopher Pence says, "the important part is the *view of the worker*. One man's labor is another's calling."

Notwithstanding this implication that meaning and purpose are to be found *in the worker*, as we have noted previously, it is difficult to deny that there are some features *in the world around work* that make some work more conducive to cultivating meaning and purpose than others. Wrzesniewski and colleagues, drawing on other organizational behavior research, suggest that stable personality traits of individuals "interact with the objective characteristics of the work." Philosopher Joanne Ciulla refers to "objective conditions" in the world around the work we do – such as the repetitiveness of the labor, the degree of autonomy that workers have to decide how to work, the hours and work schedule, and the fairness of the compensation they receive – that also influence the subjective experience of work.

As we introduced in Chapter 1, one important factor in whether we have an opportunity to work at all is what sociologist Russell Muirhead refers to as "market fit," which you may remember happens when, in a capitalist society, the skills we have to offer match up with the available employment opportunities. When there are no jobs, survival requires that we go to where the work is – which is why Fatou and her father leave their native Ivory Coast to work at a hotel in Ghana. Only a teenager, Fatou's education and experience qualify her for little more than the unskilled labor required to be a maid – an occupation that requires little more than on-the-job training. In a market economy, the pay for work that requires little expertise is usually commensurately low.

The market is one non-subjective factor that may lead us to work in one area rather than another, regardless of our subjective preferences. But, as we also reviewed in Chapter 1, philosopher Norman Care asserts that there are *moral* reasons to work, aside from *market* reasons, and that those moral reasons are the most compelling of all. He claims that, when we decide upon a career we choose between *self-realization* – fulfilling our individual aspirations and potential – and *service to others* – offering our capabilities to a world in need. Although self-realization seems like a subjective and even perhaps self-interested reason to pursue some work over other work, it is attractive to fantasize that a world in which we all felt self-realized in our work would be better in a *moral* sense too, in that every worker might feel fulfilled. Unfortunately, we live in reality, which, Care reminds us, is full of problems from environmental degradation to human suffering, meaning that those of us who have the freedom to choose our careers must attend not just to our own preferences but also the needs of others. Care says that the best kind of work involves self-realization *with* service to others but that, if we have to choose between them, we have to prioritize service to others. Morality decides for us what work we *ought to do*, even if it is not what we *wish to do*.

In Fatou's employment with the Derawals, this means that she might be the only moral person in the household when she saves the family's choking child at the expense of her personal dignity, and ultimately, the cost of her job. This also means that, like the hospital cleaners mentioned previously, meaningful work that gives back to others is not a luxury for only those in privileged professions. For Fatou, self-realization is elusive, except on those rare occasions when nobody in the Derawal family is around and she immerses herself in the health center pool. When she is there, she recalls that staff were not permitted to swim in the hotel pool back in Accra, so instead, she learned to swim in the rough waters of the sea outside the resort walls. In the comparative tranquility of the health center pool, she prides herself on her swimming ability and can forget about the daily toil that awaits her.

Subjective, Social, Normative

By this point, it should not be surprising that there is significant overlap among some of these tripartite frameworks – and the reason that such overlap exists is that they each draw upon the others and attempt to improve upon or extend the others. For example, Care's theory of career choice is originally two dimensional – self-realization and service to others – but when Christopher began teaching it in his class, his students pointed out that career choice was not entirely up to them in the marketplace to which they sometimes felt beholden.

Still, Care's suggestion that, market aside, our work opportunities exist in tension between our desires for ourselves and society's demands of us is not only a powerful philosophical proposition but representative of prevailing psychological forces. Recently, two social scientists – Douglas Lepisto and Michael Pratt – sought to examine several influential conceptions of meaningful work and found that they could be classified under two general perspectives that they termed *realization* and *justification*. Perhaps not surprisingly, they characterize realization as the "dominant" perspective in the body of scholarship they studied, and their account of what it means is consistent with – though not identical to – the conceptions of self-realization and calling that we have already encountered in the foregoing frameworks. They describe the justification perspective on meaningful work as "emerging" and assert that it seeks to answer why the work in question is "of value" – by implication, not just subjectively to the worker but also in the eyes of a society to which the value of their work may warrant justification.

Again, the idea that we work for our own self-realization or to provide value to society is powerful and important. In fact, an academic paper written by Christopher in collaboration with Michael Pratt as well as Adam Grant and Craig Dunn positions Grant's research on prosocial motivation – in a nutshell, finding self-realization in service to others – as a significant source of meaning and purpose at work. Similarly, a paper of Jen's that meta-analyzed the collected work on calling found that calling relates to overall well-being through both internal (self-realization) and external (service to others) pathways. From this perspective, meaningful work can be both *good to me* (i.e., meaningful in our own eyes) and *good to others* (i.e., meaningful in the eyes of others), as Christopher wrote in another academic paper several years later.

However, the impetus for this latter paper was ongoing debates about whether meaningfulness as good to me and/or good to others was good enough to characterize what meaningful work *ought to be* from a normative perspective. Again, for philosophers, *normative* meaning is *prescriptive*, about ideals that are independent of our descriptive experience. It seemed to Christopher that plenty of people pursue activities that are meaningful to them or even meaningful in the eyes of society that, upon examination, may warrant reconsideration.

Take Fogle, for example. As a young "wastoid," as his more mature narrator self describes his youth, he saw nothing wrong with his aimless lifestyle that was funded by his father's workaday existence as a municipal accountant. Fogle the narrator makes a point of noting about his father that, "Like many men of his generation, he may well have been one of those people who can just proceed on autopilot" – code for neither seeking nor finding meaning and purpose in his work. "I'm not sure he ever asked himself major questions like '*Do I like my job? Is this really what I want to spend my life doing? Is it as fulfilling as some of the dreams I had for myself when I was a young man?*'" Every day, the elder Fogle trudged dutifully wearing a suit and hat into a working world of which the younger Fogle wanted no part.

At the same time, it was not until after his father's death that Chris came to realize that his ability to subsist in pursuit of hedonistic pleasure depended upon his father's income from a nondescript job. The narrator's perspective on his younger self suggests that our *subjective* perspectives on what is meaningful in our youth – doing nothing – and what seems meaningless – municipal accounting – may evolve with time and maturity. That is not to say, however, that our younger selves are always wrong and our mature selves are always right. As alluded to previously, Fogle ultimately follows, to some extent, in his father's footsteps, becoming a tax accountant who works for a government entity – not out of a sense of duty, but rather out of a sensation of having found his calling. Yet part of what makes *The Pale King* such a brilliant comic novel is that nearly anyone who has not been called to tax accounting can hardly imagine that tax accounting could be a calling for anyone. Most of the rest of *The Pale King* is about boredom at work, specifically among tax accountants working for Fogle's employer, the United States Internal Revenue Service. Given the way that Fogle stumbles into his calling – and the professor's overwrought speech about heroism in mundanity that we quoted above – there is more than a little evidence that Fogle may be as mistaken that tax accounting is meaningful as he was that being a wastoid was worthwhile.

The point here is that the problem with declaring meaningful work as subjectively determined, socially conferred, or both is that we may be wrong about our personal perceptions of it or our social appraisal of it. The meaning of tax accounting in the eyes of the younger Fogle amounted to that it was his dad's job – little more. Tax accounting has an undeniable *social* purpose, to be sure, but it is generally perceived as a necessary government function from which most people recoil. When Fogle finds his calling in tax accounting, Wallace invites skepticism about whether tax accounting could possibly be significantly meaningful – that is to say, *full of meaning*. All of which begs the question: Does the work of tax accounting have meaning and purpose? It would seem judgmental, in the worst sense of the word, to declare from our position outside the profession that it does not, even though we have known and worked with plenty of tax accountants who dutifully fulfill their service to society without claiming that there is anything particularly noble about their profession. Christopher has argued that *normative meaningfulness* should be distinguished from *experienced meaningfulness*. From a normative perspective, what makes work meaningful is neither subjective perception nor social approval but something independent of them and intrinsic to the work that is not just *in the worker, in the well-being of its beneficiaries,* or *in the world* but also *in the work*. When we are right about the meaningfulness of work, it is *good to us* and *good to society* because it is *good in itself* – not the other way around.

Utility, Pleasure, Perfect

As we have noted previously, work orientations were originally described as ways in which people relate to their work. Accordingly, the next tripartite framework is about a particular type of relationship: friendship. Can a theory of friendship between people also function as a theory of relationships between people and their work?

Aristotle posited that there are three types of friendship: utility, pleasure, and perfect. The first tends to be transactional and short-lived, only lasting as long as two friends are useful to one another. There is no doubt that work involves temporary, transactional relationships between people, whether they involve cashier and customer or employer and employee. But Fatou's journey also suggests that her experience of work has been much like a utility friendship. When the threat to her personal well-being outweighed the value of her compensation, she left. And when she becomes aware of the prospect for employment as a cleaner at her friend's office, naturally, she sees that as an opportunity to solve the problem of her unemployment.

The person who suggests that she work at his office as Andrew, her only friend in London and her only escape from the Derawals other than the swimming pool. They go out for dessert and talk about work, religion, and freedom, but he always pays because she has no income. Are they so-called Platonic friends? The story is perhaps intentionally ambiguous about his romantic designs upon her, if he envisions the possibility of physical pleasure, and if she would reciprocate. Pleasure friendships, like utility friendships, only last as long as the benefits, and although romance may be one obvious kind of pleasure, going out for sweets and conversation is another form of pleasure. It is much clearer that Fatou's principal source of pleasure is the swimming pool, where one time, she sneaks Andrew in and subsequently laughs at his lack of waterborne prowess. Meanwhile, although she may dream of work that offers a sense of pleasure, her work at the Derawals is mainly one of psychological and even physical pain.

Perfect friendships are permanent and involve protagonists whose affection is mutual and who regard the other as another self. They may be willing to put the well-being of their friend on equal footing to or even ahead of their own. There is nobody in "The Embassy of Cambodia" who are obviously perfect friends, though again, the story is ambiguous about whether Andrew's and Fatou's friendship will grow. Not even the Derawals' relationship with their own children displays this kind of selflessness, as demonstrated by Mrs. Derawal's prioritization of her own pride ahead of the life of her choking child. Similarly, there are no examples of a perfect relationship to work in the story, either. However, the story ends with a hint of ironic optimism after Fatou has been fired: "Walking out into the cold gray, Fatou felt a sense of brightness, of being washed clean, that neither the weather nor her new circumstances could dim." We can imagine what is probably next – that her new place of employment will involve another utility relationship to her work – but with the measure of freedom she has gained, perhaps she will eventually find the perfect place to work. Might she find her action, her self-realization, her calling? Keep in mind, of course, that – as with perfect friendship – perfect work is not what we would like it to be at every moment and it even sometimes requires us to sacrifice ourselves for the ideals we work for. This imaginative exercise puts in the foreground a question at the core of "The Embassy of Cambodia" and the badminton game that continues on in the background: To what extent is the work we do and the meaning and purpose thereof within our control to determine and decide, and to what extent are we just like a shuttlecock, being batted back and forth by the forces around us no matter what kind of future we aspire to?

Drifter, Dreamer, Doer

Every one of the preceding theories is an *academic* theory, developed to be tested using social scientific methods or emerging from age-old philosophical contemplation of the role of work in the good life for a human being. They may have staying power because they challenge conventional wisdom – leading us, for example, to wonder whether meaning is located in the worker, the world, or the work. Or, sometimes they speak to us because they are consistent with common sense but give us a language to express what seems apparent – for example, that the same work can mean different things to different people. However, even if every one of the frameworks has some sort of explanatory value to us, they are not always consistent with each other. Moreover, they may be no substitute for so-called real-world experience – the things ordinary people see that may not require an academic theory to explain.

In the eyes of Anne Bogan – an executive secretary quoted in Studs Terkel's 1972 book *Working* – it is better to do than to dream and better to dream than to drift. Terkel's book was a journalist's exploration of American working life at a point in time much like the present in which most people have to work and have uneasy relationships to the work they do. He interviewed everyone from steel workers to sex workers and executive secretaries to the executives they served, including Bogan, who had been on the job for eight years. She forms her own tripartite framework from her front row seat at the office – a framework that describes Fogle's journey from drifter to dreamer to doer as well as any:

> I become very impatient with dreamers. I respect the doers more than the dreamers. So many people, it seems to me, talk about all the things they want to do. They only talk without accomplishing anything. The drifters are worse than the dreamers. Ones who really have no goals, no aspirations at all, just live from day to day.

Like a shuttlecock drifting in the wind, young Fogle allows the world to decide for him what his destiny will be. He is the archetypal drifter, moving from job to job and college to college, and – when he is in college – changing majors, performing poorly, and most of the time, under the influence of mind-altering substances. His more mature narrator self most often describes this period in his life as that of a "wastoid" but also admits, "I was the worst kind of nihilist – the kind who isn't even aware he's a nihilist. I was like a piece of paper on the street in the wind, thinking, 'No I think I'll blow this way, now I think I'll blow that way.'"

Nihilism can informally describe the day-to-day attitude of a drifter that nothing matters, or as Fogle puts it, "My essential response to everything was 'Whatever.'" However, it is also the name of a complex and diverse system of thought that philosophers have articulated and rearticulated through the ages that expresses a more existential concern that the human condition is devoid of meaning and purpose. The etymology of the word is derived from Latin for "nothing," and its ethos can be traced to ancient thought in multiple traditions that tend toward skepticism about some fundamental or even supernatural force that confers meaning upon human life and activity. Much as Fogle's nihilism stereotypically involves a rejection of his father's equally unreflective compliance with social convention that coerces him into workaday existence; in Ivan Turgenev's 1862 novel *Fathers and Sons*, nihilism is embraced by the younger generation to challenge the older generation's values and way of life. However, some commentators believe that perhaps philosophy's most famous nihilist, Friedrich Nietzsche, was not a nihilist after all. The German philosopher's proclamation, "God is dead," could be taken to mean that, without the moral foundation provided by a supernatural being, every kind of behavior is permitted. However, there is evidence that Nietzsche himself – whose writings were deliberately obscure and open to interpretation – intended the metaphorical death of God to give people the freedom to choose a life worth living rather than to go along uncritically with traditional norms and mores.

Comically, what awakens Fogle from his meaningless existence as a drifter is a television announcer's declaration, "You're watching *As the World Turns*," the title of a weekday afternoon soap opera that Fogle takes as a message directly to him that "You are sitting on an old yellow dorm couch, spinning a black-and-white soccer ball, and watching *As the World Turns*, without ever even acknowledging to yourself this is what you are doing." This leads him to realize, "I had somehow chosen to have nothing matter," much as French existentialist Jean-Paul Sartre declared that the alternative to *nothingness* was to exercise *being* through one's freedom to choose otherwise. A few days later, still a bit of a drifter, Fogle stumbles into the wrong classroom and encounters the Advanced Tax review session and begins to dream of a future in which he exercises his freedom to choose more than nothing. The drifter-turned-dreamer becomes a doer, buying a suit and dress shoes and studying for the CPA exam. He braves a snowstorm to get to a practically empty IRS recruiting station in the city where he is hired by an "exhausted and disheveled" recruiter whose appearance and demeanor gives the reader reason to wonder whether Fogle's fortuitous discovery of his calling as a tax accountant is really something worth celebrating.

Good, True, Beautiful

Obviously, there are many theories about what makes work meaningful. We gave more than a full chapter's worth of attention to the work orientation (job, career, calling) framework because it has been particularly influential in our shared field of management. Its explanatory power is confirmed by what it shares with several other theories of work we have shared, but its incompleteness is also revealed by what it does not share with other theories. Each framework calls out different of our relationships to work: Wrzesniewski et al.'s work orientations offer some (but not all) possible reasons we work, whereas the elements of Arendt's *vita activa* help us to understand how work can detract from or contribute to meaning and purpose. Michaelson's normative theory of meaningful work shows how meaningfulness is about more than mere subjective satisfaction and that what seemed meaningful when we were young can change with time and maturity (or vice versa). Bogan's "3D" framework provides a compelling classification not only of the workers in her office but also of Fogle's journey toward a career.

Just as there are multiple theories of work that are loosely compatible and complementary with one another, there are also many theories of meaning that do not all say the same thing. However, philosophers generally agree that meaning is to be found at the intersection of three forms of value: ethical, epistemological, and aesthetic – or what more colloquially we can refer to as the good, the true, and the beautiful. This is the final tripartite framework in this chapter that may help us make sense of the relationship between all the other tripartite frameworks.

Is beauty in the eye of the beholder? The answer to that question depends upon whether you are an aesthetic formalist – essentially, the idea that what makes some works of art or works of nature more beautiful than others is their conformity with objectively attractive properties, such as symmetry, balance of color, and so on. But, as with meaningfulness – which philosopher Susan Wolf describes as "where subjective attraction meets objective attractiveness" – even formalists admit that which is objectively beautiful (in a formal sense) ought also to be subjectively attractive (in the eye of the beholder). So, one feature that all seven of the foregoing frameworks share is some sense that meaningful work should be subjectively appealing – even beautiful. This is the case whether we are considering work orientations that imply reasons we *want to work* whether or not we love it or Pence's similar classification in which *workmanship* involves craft and artistry. The subjective experience of beauty is also, arguably, present in the ideal of finding self-realization through work and in a dreamer's imagination of future work that is more appealing than the present. There is meaning to be found in beauty or the hope for beauty in the work we do.

However, there is also meaning to be found beyond the eye of the beholder. Several, if not all, of the frameworks suggest that a substantial part of what makes work worth doing is its *goodness* in the eyes of others – often, the beneficiaries of work. This idea is particularly present in normative theories of meaningful work that include, for example, the idea that market fit is one way of determining society's wants and needs through demand for the work that must get done. This idea is also expressed in some of the descriptive theories, including the broad definition of *calling* that includes not only personal fulfillment but also societal value. In other words, all of the theories suggest that meaning and purpose is perhaps about more than one's own

Table 4.1 Frameworks of Meaning and Meaningfulness for Examining Life and Work

Source of Framework	Element 1	Element 2	Element 3
Robert Bellah et al., *Habits of the Heart*, and Amy Wrzesniewski et al., "Jobs, Careers, and Callings"	Job	Career	Calling
Hannah Arendt, *The Human Condition*	Labor	Work	Action
Gregory Pence, "Towards a Theory of Work"	Labor	Workmanship	Calling
Norman Care, "Career Choice," and Russell Muirhead, *Just Work*	Market fit	Service to others	Self-realization
Christopher Wong Michaelson, "A Normative Meaning of Meaningful Work"	Subjective	Social	Normative
Aristotle, *Nicomachean Ethics*	Utility	Pleasure	Perfect
Anne Bogan (in Terkel's *Working*)	Drifter	Dreamer	Doer
Meaning of life theory (various)	Goodness	Truth	Beauty

interests and, more often, to be found in the ways in which work can make the world a better place for everyone.

Finally, taken together, although these theories may help us to conceive and idealize about meaningful work, they are ultimately about work in the real world – *truth* – rather than hypothetical activity. This includes Arendt's characterization of *work* as leaving a permanent object but especially her *action* orientation, echoed in Bogan's preference for *doing* over *dreaming*. In the end, the fact that theories of meaningful work coalesce around the same three features of meaningful life – the good, the true, and the beautiful – suggests that they are onto something, even if none of them alone captures what meaningful work may be.

Questions and Prompts for Review and Reflection About Chapter 4

- Which is your favorite framework for understanding why people work? Why?
- Some, though not all, of these frameworks position Element 1 as inferior and Element 3 as superior. In your view, is there a hierarchy of relationships to our work from least to most desirable?
- Reflect upon Aristotle's theory of friendship. Do you work or wish to work in a workplace in which your colleagues interact as utility friends, pleasure friends, or perfect friends?
- Like Anne Bogan, do you have a theory of your own for explaining different types of workers and their relationships to their work?
- Is there an overarching work orientation framework that might capture all (or most) of these frameworks? See if you can construct one.

Chapter 4 References

Arendt, Hannah. *The Human Condition*. Chicago: University of Chicago Press, 1958.

Aristotle. *Nichomachean Ethics*. Translated by D.P. Chase, 2003. Accessed February 28, 2024. www.gutenberg.org/files/8438/8438-h/8438-h.htm#

Aristotle. *Poetics*. Translated by S.H. Butcher, 2013. Accessed September 24, 2023. www.gutenberg.org/files/1974/1974-h/1974-h.htm

Berkeley, George. *A Treatise Concerning Principles of Human Knowledge*. Indianapolis, IN: Hackett, 1982.

Boova, Laura, Michael G. Pratt, and Douglas A. Lepisto. "Exploring Work Orientations and Cultural Accounts of Work." In *The Oxford Handbook of Meaningful Work*, edited by Ruth Yeoman, Catherine Bailey, Adrian Madden, and Marc Thompson, 186–207. Oxford: Oxford University Press, 2019.

Care, Norman S. "Career Choice." *Ethics* 94, no. 2 (1984): 283–302.

Ciulla, Joanne B. *The Working Life: The Promise and Betrayal of Modern Work*. New York: Currency, 2001.

Crawford, Matthew B. *Shop Class as Soulcraft: An Inquiry Into the Value of Work*. New York: Penguin, 2009.

Dobrow, Shoshana R., Hannah Weisman, Daniel Heller, and Jennifer Tosti-Kharas. "Calling and the Good Life: A Meta-Analysis and Theoretical Extension." *Administrative Science Quarterly* 68, no. 2 (2023): 508–550. https://doi.org/10.1177/00018392231159641

Gertz, Nolan. *Nihilism*. Cambridge, MA: The MIT Press, 2019.

Lepisto, Douglas A., and Michael G. Pratt. "Meaningful Work as Realization and Justification." *Organizational Psychology Review* 7, no. 2 (2017): 99–121. https://doi.org/10.1177/2041386616630039

Mar, Raymond A. "The Neural Bases of Social Cognition and Story Comprehension." *Annual Review of Psychology* 62 (2011): 103–134.

Metz, Thaddeus. *Meaning in Life: An Analytic Study*. Oxford: Oxford University Press, 2013.

Michaelson, Christopher. "Accounting for Meaning: On §22 of David Foster Wallace's *The Pale King*." *Critical Perspectives on Accounting* 29 (2015): 54–64. https://doi.org/10.1016/j.cpa.2015.01.013

Michaelson, Christopher. "A Normative Meaning of Meaningful Work." *Journal of Business Ethics* 170 (2021): 413–428. https://doi.org/10.1007/s10551-019-04389-0

Michaelson, Christopher. "A Novel Approach to Business Ethics Education: Exploring How to Live and Work in the 21st Century." *Academy of Management Learning & Education* 15, no. 3 (2016): 588–606.

Michaelson, Christopher, Michael G. Pratt, Adam M. Grant, and Craig P. Dunn. "Meaningful Work: Connecting Business Ethics and Organization Studies." *Journal of Business Ethics* 121 (2014): 77–90. https://doi.org/10.1007/s10551-013-1675-5

Muirhead, Russell. *Just Work*. Cambridge, MA: Harvard University Press, 2007.

Nussbaum, Martha. *Upheavals of Thought: The Intelligence of Emotions*. Cambridge: Cambridge University Press, 2001.

Pence, Gregory. "Towards a Theory of Work." In *Philosophy and the Problems of Work*, edited by Kory Schaff, 93–105. Lanham, MD: Rowman & Littlefield, 2001.

Sartre, Jean-Paul. *Being and Nothingness*. Translated by Hazel E. Barnes. New York: Simon & Schuster.

Schabram, Kira, Jordan Nielsen, and Jeffery Thompson. "The Dynamics of Work Orientations: An Updated Typology and Agenda for the Study of Jobs, Careers, and Callings." *Academy of Management Annals* 17, no. 2 (2023): 405–438. https://doi.org/10.5465/annals.2021.0153

Smith, Zadie. *Changing My Mind: Occasional Essays*. New York: Penguin, 2010.

Smith, Zadie. *The Embassy of Cambodia*. London: Hamish Hamilton, 2013.

Smith-McGregor, Kilby. "Other People's Words: In Friendship." *Kenyon Review*, Fall 2014. https://kenyonreview.org/kr-online-issue/2014-fall/selections/kilby-smith-mcgregor-656342/

Solomon, Robert C., and Kathleen M. Higgins. *What Nietzsche Really Said.* New York: Pantheon, 2000.

Terkel, Studs. *Working: What People Do All Day and How They Feel About What They Do.* New York: Pantheon Books, 1974.

Turgenev, Ivan. *Fathers and Sons.* Translated by George Reavy. New York: Signet Classics, 1961.

Wallace, David Foster. *The Pale King.* New York: Little, Brown, 2011.

Wallace, David Foster. *Something to Do with Paying Attention.* New York: McNally Editions, 2011.

"What Were You Looking At? A Host of Celebrities Choose Their Books of the Year." *The Guardian.* December 15, 2000. www.theguardian.com/books/2000/dec/16/bestbooksoftheyear.bestbooks2

Wittgenstein, Ludwig. *Philosophical Investigations* (3rd edition). Translated by G.E.M. Anscombe. New York: Macmillan.

Wolf, Susan. *Meaning in Life and Why It Matters.* Princeton, NJ: Princeton University Press, 2010.

Wrzesniewski, Amy, Clark McCauley, Paul Rozin, and Barry Schwartz. "Jobs, Careers, and Callings: People's Relations to Their Work." *Journal of Research in Personality* 31, no. 1 (1997): 21–33. https://doi.org/10.1006/jrpe.1997.2162

Zak, Paul J. "How Stories Change the Brain." *Greater Good Magazine.* December 17, 2013. https://greatergood.berkeley.edu/article/item/how_stories_change_brain

5 Meaning and Purpose in Organizations
Opportunities and Challenges

Division of Labor, or Why We Work in Organizations

If you have ever held Adam Smith's *The Wealth of Nations*, you know it cannot easily fit into one hand. It is one of those long and sometimes tedious classics that many people have heard of but few have bothered to read. To the present-day sensibility, it can get verbose and even cringe-worthily Eurocentric. Yet, like it or not, it is an important book that profoundly and often invisibly affects our daily existence – such as how our workplaces are structured in such a way as to multiply our collective production well beyond what we would generate if each of us worked independently. As a foundational text for modern economic theory, it holds the key to the price of everything, including what we are paid for the labor we supply. If you want to answer the question "Why do we tend to work in organizations rather than as individuals?" you could do worse than to begin with this book.

In Chapter I, Smith describes an assembly line for the manufacture of a familiar object, the pin:

> One man draws out the wire, another straights it, a third cuts it, a fourth points it, a fifth grinds it at the top for receiving the head; to make the head requires two or three distinct operations; to put it on, is a peculiar business, to whiten the pins is another; it is even a trade by itself to put them into the paper; and the important business of making a pin is, in this manner, divided into about eighteen distinct operations, which, in some manufactories, are all performed by distinct hands.

Eighteen steps, to make a simple pin! Consider, for a moment, what that meant for the poor workers. It was dark, dirty, loud, and sometimes dangerous on an 18th-century factory floor. Moreover, they were occupied at one station on such an assembly line, specializing in just one of those 18 operations all day – nearly every day – of their working lives, at which they spent more of their waking hours than doing anything else. And you might have thought it was tedious *to read about* pin manufacturing.

DOI: 10.4324/9781003307327-5

However, that is not Smith's main point (pun intended). When it was published in 1776, *The Wealth of Nations* was rather an innovative inquiry into the productivity benefits of a form of economic organization that we now recognize as capitalism. Among other things, a key feature of capitalism that Smith celebrated and that endures today is the division of labor. This division is illustrated in the distinct stages of pin manufacturing. One of the reasons that division of labor works on the assembly line is that each worker becomes more expert at a particular task than they otherwise would if they had to master 18 of them in succession.

As we have already seen, meaningfulness is sometimes described as a sense of participating in something bigger than ourselves. If you think about it, that is the very essence of working within an organization. Smith observed that 18 stations working in harmony were more productive by many multiples than 18 stations working in isolation from one another, so in that sense, it may be said that participating in efficient production is meaningful. Whether making pins, farming food, building buildings, or sending spaceships into orbit, many, if not most, business activities would be impossible to achieve at scale without the organization to, well, organize and harness the power of many to do something big together that matters.

If that is the point of working in an organization, however, then why does working on an assembly line tend to make workers feel small and insignificant, as though they do not matter? Going back to job characteristics theory, assembly line workers in the Industrial Revolution had small jobs: little to no autonomy, working on only a small part of the final product, and often receiving little to no recognition for their work; only the avoidance of punishment should they fall behind. Scientific management, designed by engineer Frederick Taylor at the turn of the 20th century, sought to train men to be as efficient as machines, and the human emotion that accompanied such roles might have reflected this. Adam Smith himself observed that the value of specialization exacts a cost on workers' lives not accounted for in the economic price of work. Toward the end of *The Wealth of Nations*, he laments:

> The man whose whole life is spent in performing a few simple operations, of which the effects too are, perhaps, always the same, or very nearly the same, has no occasion to exert his understanding, or to exercise his invention in finding out expedients for removing difficulties which never occur. He naturally loses, therefore, the habit of such exertion, and generally *becomes as stupid and ignorant as it is possible for a human creature to become.*

> (emphasis added)

As a critical factor in why we are more productive in organizations than as isolated individuals, division of labor also helps to explain why many modern human beings with otherwise interesting inner lives and aspirations and the wherewithal to choose their line of work often feel stuck, in a metaphorical or even literal sweatshop, pursuing uninspiring careers that have little value to them other than the money that compensates them for their daily misery.

Work on a Modern, White-Collar Assembly Line

In the centuries since Smith touted the productive potential of industrializing markets, most of the world's nations have modernized their economies, realizing growth in GDP per capita coinciding with industrialization. Critics note that the absolute benefits of this increase in wealth have not necessarily conferred benefits equitably and that industrial economies have imposed costs upon future generations. Smith's views on the differences between agrarian economies and industrial ones and the relationship between them are complex and controversial, but suffice it to say for our purposes that he observed some of the same productivity benefits of division of labor on farms as in factories – as well as some costs. With division of labor came a divide between owners of capital and labor as the means of production, as capitalists say, which led over time to not only different roles and responsibilities but different places and paradigms of work. What are known today as "blue-collar" jobs subsist on farms and factory floors involving manual labor, whereas so-called "white-collar" jobs take place in offices on high floors of skyscrapers from which factory floors can neither literally nor figuratively be seen except in representations as numbers on spreadsheets. The quintessential manual laborer has scarce room to grow and advance as a professional. As Lynn Nottage's *Sweat* – a Pulitzer prize-winning play about steelworkers in the throes of the Great Recession – suggests, on those rare occasions when manual laborers are promoted to the management ranks, they risk the ire of their former peers for becoming traitors of the working class. In the play, an invisible management class presses union negotiators for contract concessions before replacing them with lower-paid non-union labor, while one middle manager stands by helplessly with neither the power to change management's decisions nor to persuade her former colleagues that the actions were not her doing.

By contrast, white-collar professions are perceived to be all about advancement and associated growth of one's earning potential. The figurative phrase "climbing the career ladder" is often accompanied by promotion to higher floors of the skyscraper, a corresponding increase in pay, and the trappings of status and meaning that impressed us early in our own careers – the potential for a corner window office, fine furniture, and other symbols of success. In the 20th century, the capitalist ideal was to be an organization or "company man" – usually a man who stayed with the same employer practically from graduation to retirement, working his way up the hierarchy until receiving a gold watch with a corporate logo when his career was over. The stability of such a career has become mostly a relic of the past as career mobility has increased in the past few decades, but when we were with our consulting firms at the turn of the 21st century, it was typical that the highest officers of our firms had "grown up" within them, starting at the bottom and advancing to the top. At the time, the long hours and comparatively low salaries of newer staff in comparison to the partners who owned and operated our firms were seen as the price one had to pay to have a chance at the prize of partnership – so much so that firms like ours were characterized by Jill Andresky Fraser as "white-collar sweatshops." Different as they were from factory floors of the 18th century, they were not as different as we may arrogantly have wished to believe.

Some assembly lines like the one that Smith described centuries ago have reputations as sweatshops and still subsist in the world today – emblems of persistent exploitation of workers for whom work is a means to the end of material survival. Often, sweatshop employees have to choose between bad work and no work at all, and they have little power in the workplace to choose what to do, how to do it, when, how many hours, and how much it earns. When we compare the subjective experience of white-collar workers in relatively lucrative professions to the potential abuse endured by workers on the factory floor, we do not mean to make light of the objective conditions experienced by real sweatshop workers. Rather, we make the comparison to emphasize the irony that even people who possess the relative power and privilege to choose their own work – and the potential to influence the conditions of others' work – are also, to a certain extent, compelled to specialize at dull and demeaning tasks by the dynamics of division of labor and to inflict the dirty work on to their perceived inferiors.

As a case in point, Christopher remembers rejoicing with his colleagues when their firm was hired by an international development bank to manage its financial disclosure process. If this sounds like a boring and inscrutable assignment, it was, but it was performed in service to the higher though not entirely uncontroversial purpose of weeding out corruption while – to mix metaphors – greasing the wheels of global capitalism. The consultants were to be responsible for examining the decisions of bank officials – who authorized loans from developed countries to developing ones that were supposed to drive economic growth and infrastructure development to improve people's lives – to ensure that those decisions were made in the best interest of the recipient countries rather than the officials' own pocketbooks. Being selected for this purpose made the consultants feel important. Moreover, they had been conditioned to call any new source of client revenue a "win." Who doesn't enjoy winning – especially within the camaraderie of colleagues that have been spending late nights together grinding out multiple versions of a proposal and practicing for a presentation to the client's board in preparation for this moment? The victors toasted at a celebratory meal, booked the project in their sales tracking system that would burnish each of their year-end bonuses, and then set about planning to deliver upon the promises they had sold.

Predictably, as Motörhead sings of youthful romance, the chase was better than the catch: Being awarded the work turned out to be far more exhilarating than having actually to perform it. The work consisted of a painstaking process of comparing lengthy lists of investment holdings in the financial portfolios of bank officials alongside their job responsibilities to identify potential conflicts of interest that sometimes required tense meetings with bank officials, who bristled at being accused of the prospect of being untrustworthy. The bank was so sensitive about confidentiality that all of the files had to remain on the premises within a locked, windowless conference room where the consultants would perform their examination one, two, or no more than three at a time because they could not fit any more staff in the cramped space. It was like looking for a needle in a haystack day after day and then, on those rare occasions when a needle was located, being pricked by that very needle when the staff had to put a financial disclosure meeting on the calendar of a bank official who believed they had more important things to attend to. To accomplish the work more efficiently, the partner and manager who met with the bank officials only flew in occasionally for those meetings and to supervise the staff who performed the bulk of the detail work from their secure, interior office from which they would never see the light of day.

Although this client's specific needs may have been exceptional, the skills the project involved were typical of why Big Four professional services firms are hired by their clients: low-level, lower-rate-per-hour staff who are good at working with numbers, attending to detail, and exercising professional skepticism to support more senior, highly paid managers and partners who bring the experience and expertise to assure the client that work that it cannot perform for itself is in good hands. These firms perennially make *Fortune*'s "Best Companies to Work For" list, renowned as inclusive professional training grounds that offset the demands of hard work with flexibility and generous benefits and compensation. Traditionally, making partner – joining a fraternity-like club of shareowners into which just a small fraction of staff is admitted each year – has promised wealth, prestige, and early retirement – as well as the freedom to supervise staff performing the most dull and demeaning tasks instead of having to perform it oneself. Nevertheless, because of the boredom inherent in so much of the work, the firms have, over the years, struggled to retain some of their most promising young professionals. They would recoil at the prospect of years of manual ticking and tying – the mundane matching of debits, credits, and other minutiae to transaction and control logs – that long constituted the formative experience of early-career accountants and consultants.

As we discussed in the preceding two chapters, meaningful work, as it relates to individuals, is typically studied as a subjective phenomenon. That is to say that meaningfulness is perceived to be in the eye of the beholder. In this regard, the same ticking and tying that is dreaded by one entry-level accountant may be embraced by an aspiring partner performing the same work with a different sense of purpose. The former is endeavoring to make it through the day, while the latter has their eye on a longer-term prize. To return to the characterization of these kinds of workplaces as "white-collar sweatshops" brings attention to the relationship between the so-called "objective" conditions of work and the subjective experience thereof. As in genuine sweatshops, those objective conditions can include a long workday, the imposition of work methods by management that supports uniformity of output but stifles individual creativity, and exposure to only a small part of the production process such that the sweatshop worker never enjoys the satisfaction of completing a finished product. Limited autonomy on the part of the worker to influence the objective conditions of work can affect their potential to derive meaning from working in a subjective sense.

After a few cycles of performing the financial disclosure project for the bank, the staff developed technological tools to diminish the manual labor involved in the examination of financial disclosure files. The partner and manager on the project tried to maintain some *esprit de corps* by reminding the staff of the higher purposes for which this work was performed – their own promotion possibilities or a more equitable future for global capitalism free of corruption and fraud. However, none of this happened before some of the staff on the project had already left for pastures that they perceived as greener – one aspired to be a church singer, another to become a political science professor, and yet another to be an aid worker in the very countries to which the bank lent money.

Shifting Values: From Production, Profit, and Partnership to Purpose

This true story – some details have been modified for confidentiality and simplicity – occurred in a timely context, when both attitudes toward work and work itself were changing. The higher purpose of equitable capitalism was not high enough for the associates locked in the windowless conference room who were not willing to wait to experience the sensation of meaningful work. At the same time, artificial intelligence and other forms of technology were making their work easier while simultaneously calling the associates' value into question if they could be replaced by technology. Timely though these changes may be, this story also raises universal and timeless questions that might occur to any thoughtful person concerned that working for a living too often means working at the expense of living: What is the value of work?

The answer to this question depends upon, among other things, the perspective and position of the person answering it. Perspective has to do with the worldview that influences what you consider to be valuable. The prevailing worldview in these firms is economic, shaped by the accountants whose professional expertise concerns the assignment of a price to everything worth comparing on a balance sheet – such as securities, natural resources, and human labor. Arguably, we all value money to a certain pragmatic extent to fulfill basic needs, but those whose worldviews are dominated by economic considerations often suppose that economic factors are determinative; that is, that all value ultimately reduces to money. Even the non-accountants in a firm run by accountants become conditioned to the regularity of the rhythm with which financial reports are generated as evidence of individual and organizational value. In the purest version of this worldview, the purpose of a firm in which everything that counts can be counted is to make more of that which can be measured; that is, money.

To attract and retain talent, the Big Four have had to rethink their recruiting and human resource practices, including all of them recently adopting inspiring statements of purpose in lock step with each other. They set forth idealistic claims about the impact of the firms' work, the reality of which involves some prosaic variation on preparing financial and tax statements and providing arms and legs to support a client's large scale technology conversion. To entice young professionals who fear that to turn their professional lives over to one of these giants is to sell out on their youthful ideals, the firms profess to grandiose purposes that purport to "matter to our clients, our people, our communities" (Deloitte); "buil[d] a better working world" (EY); "empower change" (KPMG); and "build trust in society" (PwC). One function of these purpose statements is to connect the small tasks that constitute the daily work of staff – ticking and tying – to a larger end goal – greasing the wheels of a more equitable global capitalism. It can be a long way from the ground floor of these firms to these lofty aspirations, however. On the inside, daily existence may vacillate between the constant pressure to produce imposed by partners and managers who seem to be driven solely by the immediate purpose of generating billable hours and the transformational messaging from on high that continues to promise that serving the purpose of the firm is meaningful work.

It was no coincidence that all of the Big Four firms articulated grandiose statements of purpose at the same time as each other, amid a growing chorus of other businesses also claiming their own purposes, during the emergence of a what has been termed the "purpose economy" by Aaron Hurst and the "passion economy" by Adam Davidson. So, Coca-Cola "refresh[es] the world, and make[s] a difference," and Facebook "bring[s] the world closer together." The leaders of these firms, in part, wanted to recruit and retain a new generation of staff that hailed from what had been described as the "purpose generation." They were also looking over their shoulders at what their competitors were doing to ensure that they were not outmaneuvered in their quest for growth. Cynically, the idea that the raison d'être of these firms is anything other than to maximize the share values of their owners is a shrewd business strategy concocted by leaders whose entire careers have been devoted to devising business strategies to maximize their share values. Does this hypocrisy ring true with employees, for whom a purpose to work might be a motivating factor? Or does it help to justify the quest for value creation under the guise of something more noble?

Less cynically, the expression of purpose statements, at least in the Big Four, was the culmination of a gradual chipping away at the accountant's narrow, economic worldview. A few decades earlier, accountants whose primary occupation was the certification of financial accounting reports had begun to experiment with something called non-financial reporting, which purported to measure the environmental and social effects of corporate activity in balance with their economic effects – what is often termed "ESG [environmental, social, governance] reporting" in today's terms. Although non-financial reporting still expressed everything in quantifiable terms, the very acknowledgement that there were non-economic effects of business activity was a notable shift from an exclusive obsession with financial statements as the sole measure of business success – and a business opportunity for the firms to expand their reach. At the same time, the conventional, 20th-century wisdom about the purpose of the business corporation as maximizing stockholder value – captured succinctly in Milton Friedman's seminal article, "The Social Responsibility of Business is to Increase its Profits" – was giving way to a 21st-century story that the purpose of business was to create value for all stakeholders – including employees, communities, and the environment, in addition to stockholders. In 2019, the Business Roundtable – an organization composed of the CEOs of some of America's largest corporations – formalized R. Edward Freeman's formulation of stakeholder theory in its declaration of its own members' organizational purposes.

During this gradual "value shift," as Lynn Sharp Paine referred to it in her 2004 book of that title, dissatisfied with spending long hours in interior cubicles illuminated by only the artificial lighting buzzing above them, Big Four staff would sometimes open the dark cherry-wood doors to unoccupied partners' offices to let sunlight into their spaces. In some firms' offices, this led eventually to floor-by-floor renovations in which the partners' quarters and staff cubicles switched places. Since the partners were constantly on the road anyway, they settled for interior windows so that the administrative assistants and staff could see the world outside from which they were barricaded by work.

While the partners still wore power suits on airplanes, the staff who stayed behind were invited first to dress in "business casual," then for "Jeans Friday," followed by "dress for your day" policies that reflected the generational demise of professional attire. The point of these stories is to suggest that the economic view of the value of work that emphasizes productivity and profit as its only measures has given way to non-economic conceptions of the value of work in the form of purpose and personal expression. We do not deny that money cannot buy meaning any less than it can buy happiness. However, in the language of philosophers, money is an intermediate good that, though it may not be an end in itself, can be a useful means to other meaningful ends. A certain amount of money may be necessary to other ends – to support basic material needs – but it is worth considering how much money we need. In the Big Four, that realization among emerging employees has meant that many capable staff are no longer motivated to join a partnership that is primarily characterized by its economic benefits at the expense of other meaningful, non-economic aspirations.

Yet, notwithstanding their cultural inclinations toward the economic worldview, the Big Four firms' purpose statements point to non-economic goods that have value regardless of their economic standing – such as their ability to have a positive impact on their "communities" and "a better . . . world" and to make "change" and "build trust." Even the professionals who excel at accounting for "intangible value" have a hard time putting a price on these "moral sentiments," as Adam Smith called them. Although *The Wealth of Nations* is the source of Smith's enduring reputation in the capitalist global economy of the present, economists and ethicists who have studied Smith's career put that book alongside *The Theory of Moral Sentiments* as his dueling masterworks in their respective disciplines. Whereas *Wealth* is now known for suggesting that the responsibility of market actors is to pursue their self-interest and the market will work out the rest, *Sentiments* argues that market actors are neither amoral nor immoral, and self-interest is not necessarily selfish. Putting both of Smith's treatises together, this is to say that markets have a meaningfully moral purpose of supplying the world's demand. This worldview suggests that the value of work to the individuals who work in organizations connects to that moral purpose – in the form of work that has value in relation to its capacity to fulfill what other market actors need and want.

The value we ascribe to work is also influenced by our position. Naturally, the partners at the top of these firms' hierarchies who are quite economically well-off may be more favorably inclined to measure the value of work in financial terms, seeing the purpose of the firm as to make money. Meanwhile, the staff doing the lesser tasks who also lack the economic status of the top earners and the job security of a part-owner may be inspired by a moral purpose that explains what their hard work is for. They tend to wonder about the measurable and unmeasurable costs to their own aspirations and ambitions imposed by the burdens of work. The economic worldview might provide a convenient answer to the question of the value of work in a common currency. However, for the associates who had the least freedom to choose what and how to work, it also leaves essential questions unanswered about the non-economic costs and benefits that work can have for our individual chance to live a meaningful life and work at meaningful work.

These questions point to both the promise and peril of purpose. The promise is that the organizations in which we often work can fulfill those inspiring purposes, from serving society's needs to making the world a better place. They can do so at a scale that we could not achieve as individuals, harnessing collective power that enables us to connect our personal meaning and talent to a larger purpose. When management is sincere about that purpose, a purpose statement can be a managerial instrument for illuminating the connection between work in the objectively unpleasant trenches and the subjectively inspirational experience of meaningfulness. Even when economically motivated managers employ staff who care about working for a moral purpose, economic sense and moral sentiments can align together to build organizations that are monetarily successful and provide work that is meaningful to their employees. However, the potential peril arises when management insincerely embraces purpose as a marketing ploy. In such circumstances, a purpose statement can be a manipulative tool for placating staff who want to believe they have joined an organization with a reason for being greater than money and larger than they could achieve by themselves.

How Organizations Can Help Employees Create Meaning and Purpose

The structure and culture of professional services firms are a mirror into modern capitalism. In technical terms, the defining feature of capitalism is private ownership of the means of production. In practical terms, this means that owners invest their economic assets to grow the output of labor and other resources, thereby increasing their wealth. In the context of our portrayal, this means that the partner-owners use the financial fortunes they have made from their comparatively long tenures with their firms to employ new staff – who sometimes have superior educational qualifications to their elders – to carry out the labor for which staff are paid significantly less than the increase that partner share values will see as a result of that labor. The main claim that these partners have to justify their larger take from the labor of others is their willingness to put their capital at risk to a career-long sentence of overseeing labor that they no longer wish to or are even able to perform. This is not to claim that owners, in these firms or elsewhere, are undeserving of their standing. Rather, it is to suggest that the advantage that enables owners to wield power over laborers has some of the time to do with hard work and talent and at other times can be arbitrary, accidental, and even unfair.

From the very beginning of one's career in these firms, the value of quantifiable production is emphasized in the form of "utilization," the primary way in which staff performance is measured. Utilization is expressed as a percentage of one's hours that are billable to a client, much as in a pin factory utilization can express what percentage of time a machine used for polishing or soldering a pin is active – rather than undergoing maintenance or repair. In professional services, 100% utilization is equivalent to 2,016 annual hours, the contemporary definition of full-time employment. However, since vacation may be included in the base figure, along with Continuing Professional Education for accountants, plus a large share of one's time spent in team-building, strategy, sales and marketing, commuting to distant client sites, and other forms of non-billable activities – not to mention the pressure to "eat hours" to stay within budget – to reach 100% utilization often requires working 150%+ of a full-time equivalent. Achieving your utilization target makes you "time macho," Ann-Marie Slaughter's term for the unceasing, relentless pressure on upwardly mobile professionals to achieve the unachievable to demonstrate their fitness to compete. As you work your way up to partner, utilization targets diminish while a second, objectively measurable metric looms: revenue generation. Partners sell projects that generate sales revenue so that staff can deliver them to generate utilization, which yields the collection of that revenue.

How this monetary logic adds up to meaningful logic is another question. One way to determine one's meaningful contribution to the work product is to measure the investment of time and energy. Staff expend many more hours on these projects, arguably playing a more meaningful role in the outcome than the partner. In this scenario, those who invest the most meaningful effort take away the least monetary reward. This perspective has been justified by the libertarian author Ayn Rand, who reputedly claimed that the leader's disproportionate reward should be regarded as compensation for the greater risk they take on with their resources and reputation, not to mention the relative stress they experience overseeing the work of many rather than taking responsibility for the work of one. For the staff, the satisfaction of doing the work must be its own reward.

This logic may be unpersuasive to the staff who never see the full, finished product of their efforts and who are not invited to the meeting at which the client expresses its appreciation for a job well done. From this perspective, meaningfulness is located in the outcome, not the input, of the effort. The staff experience what the socialist political economist Karl Marx referred to as "alienated labor," when workers' subjective experience is so distant from the object of their work that they have no sense of ownership, figurative or literal, in it. Management scholars refer to the satisfaction of seeing a job through from start to finish as "task identity," stemming back to job characteristics theory, which, in a previous chapter, we mentioned involves the sense of meaningful identification with one's work. According to Marx, the absence thereof is the necessary condition of the capitalist industrial complex that rewards owners twofold with greater monetary capital and meaningful reward while laborers toil away in anonymity.

Of course, there is an alternative to working in the Big Four. We can see a clear contrast between the leveraged alienation of work in accounting and the experience of working for a company whose purpose is baked into everything it does (here, the pun is most definitely intended). King Arthur Flour is a 200+ year-old organization based in Vermont. Employees bought the company in 2004, and it became a certified B Corp, or benefit corporation, three years later. The B Corp distinction means that companies like KAF adhere not only to the typical assessments of profitability but also to metrics around environmental and social health. Along with Peloton, the purveyor of stationary exercise bikes, and Zoom, the platform for web meetings, King Arthur saw its sales skyrocket during the pandemic, as would-be sourdough bread bakers flocked to its flours, seasonings, and other kitchen ingredients, tools, and gadgets. One could even, if sufficiently motivated, purchase one's own sourdough starter, described on the KAF website as having been "lovingly nurtured here in New England for decades." King Arthur's ownership structure does not differentiate between partners and employees. All employees share in the company's profits directly and help decide to which causes the company will donate additional profits. These causes tend to be those that emphasize social justice, environmental stewardship, and employee wellness. Employees receive 40 hours of time per year to volunteer for a cause that is close to them. KAF files an annual impact report that involves metrics for belongingness and inclusion among employee-owners, prioritizing diverse and sustainable suppliers and partners, and meeting environmental goals like zero landfill waste and using 100% renewable flour. It is, in short, as purposeful a company as one can imagine, and every aspect of their corporate structure, culture, reward system, and supply chain has been designed to be in line with their slogan: "to let good rise." Of course, employees at King Arthur Flour are not making Big Four salaries and bonuses, even in a banner pandemic year. Then again, salaries in Vermont go at least twice as far as those in Manhattan. A cost calculator estimates that housing is 75% less expensive, not to mention that KAF has been on the "Best Places to Work in Vermont" list since 2006. As is often the case, part of the reward of deeply meaningful work is non-monetary.

A company like KAF practices what it preaches, and employees are expected to notice and remain loyal to the company in turn. In fact, employees are highly sensitive to whether the values that their employing organizations espouse are the same as those that they enact. When organizational values are in line with their own personal values, employees will go above and beyond to perform their work in the organization. They will even go above and beyond to perform work that is meaningful to them, such as pro-environmental behavior, even if not required by the company. One study found that employees' perceptions of how sustainably their company behaved mattered more than how the company actually acted in terms of informing how they felt about the company. Another study found that employees were more likely to behave in an environmentally sustainable way at work when they believed their employer valued this behavior. In fact, employees' perceptions of their employers' values mattered even more than even their *own personal values* in determining their behavior. This means that employees are constantly scanning their organizational surroundings to assess what the company truly seems to value, and therefore, how they, in turn, should act. It also means that lip service to a purpose, mission, and shared values alone will only go so far to motivate the employees to whom purpose matters most. Hypocritical purpose statements will likely be viewed as such – the internal equivalent of "greenwashing" a product to seem environmentally sound to customers – and employees will act accordingly. Employees also notice when their organizations show genuine support for their own values and efforts and consider whether their employees value their contributions toward sustainability, for example, when determining how much to actually contribute. This, in turn, means that organizations who recognize and support employee initiatives may find themselves richly rewarded in terms of employee commitment, proactive behavior, and job satisfaction.

All of this also means that the leader's role in maintaining this sense of organizational authenticity is critical. Employees typically look to their leaders' actions as symbolic of the values of the whole organization. What they say is important, but what they actually do is equally so. An example of how far employees will go to support a leader who cares about them and shares their values can be found in the regional U.S. grocery store chain, Market Basket. We are used to employees striking against management that doesn't support them, but Market Basket's cashiers, deli clerks, produce stockers, and even store managers went on strike in support of their top management. Specifically, they went on a month-long strike to protest the firing of their beloved CEO, Arthur T. Demoulas, known affectionately as "Artie T" by the Market Basket board. Artie T was known for embodying the Market Basket motto – and oft-repeated chant during the strike – "We're in the grocery business second, the people business first," in a way his successor was not. Employees ultimately prevailed, and Artie bought back the company. This feat was all the more impressive because there was no labor union backing the striking employees. Yet, they risked it all: their paychecks (for a month!), job security, and even the company they valued, for a leader who seemed to support them.

What Organizations Owe to Employees

Admittedly, it has been more than a few years since we spent the formative years of our own careers in firms like the Big Four. Although, between us, we spent more than 20 years with these firms, they underwent substantial change while we were there and since we departed. Even the earlier story about the financial disclosure team, only two decades later, is old news. The work of an entry-level accountant has evolved to the point at which augmenting human skill with artificial intelligence has become a daily reality, and the relentless travel of partners and staff has been challenged by a global pandemic. Someday, the top positions in these organizations will belong to a generation of partners who began their careers guided by their firms' purpose statements – not by a legacy generation of partners for whom the statements were developed as the latest employee engagement and retention strategy – and therefore can hopefully authentically signal to employees that these statements are authentic. However, as the parallels between pin-manufacturing and ticking and tying demonstrates, there are some enduring features of work in capitalism that shape our opportunities to partake of work in an organization – whether we work in a factory, a Big Four firm, a worker-owned B-Corp, a family business, or myriad other organizational forms.

Arguably, however, the preponderance of those who stay and work their way up to partnership in the kinds of firms we worked for are not born for this work, but rather made for it. That is, they are shaped by their firm's way of doing business that causes their identities to become indistinguishable from the prevailing worldview that imposes constraints on their conception of what is meaningful. They learn, for example, from the accountants that everything – from measurable time to unmeasurable brand management and business development – should be tracked and monetized and subject to a return-on-investment calculation. They discover that their own utilization and revenue generation scores are the primary determinants of candidacy for promotion and partner. We encountered many people in our firms and their clients who found the pursuit of money to be a thrilling end in itself, who would revel in the competition and bask in its rewards. They were often charismatic, intelligent, enjoyable colleagues to work with who had a magnetic ability to recruit staff to join them in the pursuit. However, for every such person, there was another who could not wait to escape a world in which revenue generation was the measure of your worth not just as a worker but also, it sometimes seemed, as a human being. No matter how hard you worked or how talented you were, every day was an exercise in recording your time in increments of tenths of an hour and with the end of every semi-monthly time period came reminders of new prospects, recent sales, and revenue collections. In the process, they were conditioned to persist through sometimes difficult and deleterious tasks and to endure intense pressure and long hours because that is all that anyone else at their level and above them knows. When pressed to think about the broader purpose of what the firms did, it was hard to escape the phrase "Making the rich richer"; unclear whether and how clients were working to serve nobler ends. Most of these firms' senior management have been so immersed in this water that they cannot even recognize that there is a world above the surface full of alternative ways of working and living. Only the staff who temporarily occupy the firmament between this water and the world above have the wherewithal to wonder if this work is worth the kind of lifestyle it demands.

We do not mean to suggest that our own experiences working in this environment were bad; quite the contrary. There is also something intoxicating about being a globetrotter; to discover that someone needs you to fly to them to help them solve a problem that they cannot fix by themselves. There is fun in visiting new places, racking up loyalty rewards points, and staying in hotels . . . at first! As you advance up the ladder, you are no longer responsible for working so much as you are observing the work of many others beneath you in the pyramid, consulted on only the most important and momentous decisions. And, of course, selling work whenever and wherever possible. No matter where you are in the pyramid, you are part of a leveraged machine that is bigger than yourself and more productive than you could ever hope to be on your own. You can solve problems that only a super-human combination of ingenuity and expertise can solve and make legions of metaphorical pins in a day instead of a paltry few. Money aside, for many of us, meaning consists of exactly that: participating in a community working together for a shared purpose that is bigger than what we could have dreamed up by ourselves. Contributing to the productivity of one of the world's largest and most prestigious firms lends meaning in the form of status and recognition to each act of work that constitutes a contribution, whoever we are. Working so hard and winning together means your work colleagues become your work friends and potentially even your partners.

Our purpose in sharing these stories is to relate the burden of being a capitalist that is concomitant with the material rewards. It is to recognize and respect that there are people who, for reasons material and immaterial, choose or get chosen for this lifestyle, for better or worse. It is to be mindful of our own potential power to influence not only the value and meaning of our own work but also the work and well-being of our employees and others throughout the value chain. It is to facilitate choice, not to stand in the way of it. As we have noted, one of the benefits of making partner in one of these firms is the promise of an early and rich retirement. To make room for new partners, mandatory retirement often kicks in when the older partners are in their 50's, after which retired partners typically go on to do what they really wished all along to do with a comfortable pension – whether it is to see their families, see the world, or see if they can succeed at an encore career.

We were not willing to wait that long to do what we really wanted to do. Jen left fairly suddenly after 9/11, enrolling in graduate school to pursue her doctorate in management. Christopher left slowly, landing his first position as a full-time lecturer the following fall but keeping a part-time foot in his former firm for almost 15 more years. In this respect, one important difference between the pin-manufacturing assembly line and the professional-services assembly line is the degree of economic freedom to choose whether to work, which is often tied to the degree of educational freedom to choose which work to do. We both took dramatic pay cuts to pursue academic positions, and though the money was enticing, we had the economic privilege – from our savings from these jobs and families who would catch us if we fell – and the educational privilege – our potential for future professional success in our new jobs – such that money was not the decisive factor for us.

That privilege has opened our eyes not only to the opportunities for meaning and purpose that organizations provide us but also to the obstacles they present that in turn suggest moral obligations to provide work with a purpose or at least to preserve workers' ability to pursue work that is meaningful to them. As the previous stories suggest, owners of organizations can use laborers as a means of production, letting them do the dirty work while exploiting them as levers for their own multiplying rewards. Philosopher Adina Schwartz describes the pin-manufacturing story as one in which "workers are in effect paid for blindly pursuing ends that others have chosen, by means that they judge adequate," contending that organizations have moral responsibilities to give their employees – especially those who do not have the wherewithal to choose to leave – the autonomy to choose why and how to do their work. Other philosophers have added various other moral conditions to organizations, including but not limited the right to free entry and exit, a limit on hours, and a decent wage – though philosopher Robert Nozick has argued that the meaningless work may be the price we pay for the monetary compensation we receive in return. That debate seems to sum up the fundamental question that we began with regarding why we work in organizations. Does it add meaning and purpose to our lives, or does it detract from them in a way that demands compensation and protection? The answer to that question may depend upon the leaders we work for – and the leaders we are determined to become.

Questions and Prompts for Review and Reflection About Chapter 5

- Consider your work or your academic discipline of study. How does the way in which your work role and/or your academic discipline is defined reflect the way in which division of labor demands specialization in the form of excellence in a particular role or discipline?
- Do you think it is fair that, from historical factory floors to modern professional services firms, owners of capital tend to earn more than the workers who constitute means of production? Why or why not?
- Imagine a need you have identified in society or a problem that you would like to solve. How might working as part of an organization enable you to achieve your goal more efficiently and effectively working on your own?
- Make a pros and cons list of the perceived advantages and disadvantages of working in the kinds of firms in which we used to work. How enticing is the prospect of working there to you?
- How does working in organizations potentially give meaning and purpose to our work? How does working in organizations potentially take meaning and purpose away from our work?

Chapter 5 References

Andresky Fraser, Jill. *White Collar Sweatshop: The Deterioration of Work and Its Rewards in Corporate America*. New York: W. W. Norton & Co, 2001.

CNN Money. "Cost of Living: How Far Will My Salary Go in Another City?" Accessed February 26, 2024. https://money.cnn.com/calculator/pf/cost-of-living/index.html

Freeman, R. Edward. "The New Story of Business: Towards a More Responsible Capitalism." *Business and Society Review* 122, no. 3 (Fall 2017): 449–465. https://doi.org/10.1111/basr.12123

Friedman, Milton. "A Friedman Doctrine: The Social Responsibility of Business Is to Increase Its Profits." *The New York Times*. September 13, 1970. www.nytimes.com/1970/09/13/archives/a-friedman-doctrine-the-social-responsibility-of-business-is-to.html

Glavas, Ante, and Lindsey N. Godwin. "Is the Perception of 'Goodness' Good Enough? Exploring the Relationship Between Perceived Corporate Social Responsibility and Employee Organizational Identification." *Journal of Business Ethics* 114 (2013): 15–27. https://doi.org/10.1007/s10551-012-1323-5

Gow, Ian D., and Stuart Kells. *The Big Four: The Curious Past and Perilous Future of the Global Accounting Monopoly*. Oakland, CA: Berrett-Koehler, 2018.

King Arthur Baking. "2022 Impact Report." Accessed February 26, 2024. www.kingarthurbaking.com/impact/impact-report

Lamm, Eric, Jennifer Tosti-Kharas, and Cynthia E. King. "Empowering Employee Sustainability: Perceived Organizational Support Toward the Environment." *Journal of Business Ethics* 128 (2015): 207–220. https://doi.org/10.1007/s10551-014-2093-z

Marx, Karl. "Estranged Labor." Translated by Martin Mulligan. *Economic and Philosophical Manuscripts of 1844*. Accessed from Marxist.org, February 26, 2024. www.marxists.org/archive/marx/works/1844/manuscripts/labour.htm

McCarron, Meghan. "The Year Flour Was King." *Eater*. December 21, 2020. www.eater.com/22178960/king-arthur-flour-supply-chain-baking-boom

McNally, David. *Political Economy and the Rise of Capitalism: A Reinterpretation*. Berkeley, CA: University of California Press, 1988.

Nottage, Lynn. *Sweat (TCG Edition)*. New York: Theatre Communications Group, 2017.

Nozick, Robert. *Anarchy, State, and Utopia*. New York: Basic Books, 2013.

Paine, Lynn Sharp. *Value Shift: Why Companies Must Merge Social and Financial Imperatives to Achieve Superior Performance*. New York: McGraw-Hill, 2004.

Piketty, Thomas. *Capital in the Twenty-First Century*. Translated by Arthur Goldhammer. Cambridge, MA: Harvard University Press, 2014.

Sampson, Anthony. *Company Man: The Rise and Fall of Corporate Life*. New York: Crown Business, 1995.

Schwartz, Adina. "Meaningful Work." *Ethics* 92, no. 4 (1982): 634–646. www.jstor.org/stable/2380395

Slaughter, Anne-Marie. "Why Women Still Can't Have It All." *The Atlantic*. July/August 2012. Accessed July 27, 2023. www.theatlantic.com/magazine/archive/2012/07/why-women-still-cant-have-it-all/309020/

Smith, Adam. *An Inquiry into the Nature and Causes of the Wealth of Nations*. New York: Bantam Dell, 2003.

Smith, Adam. *The Theory of Moral Sentiments*. New York: Penguin Classics, 2010.

Solman, Paul. "With Jobs on the Line, Why Are Market Basket Employees So Loyal to Artie T?" *PBS NewsHour*. August 13, 2014. www.pbs.org/newshour/nation/with-jobs-on-the-line-why-are-market-basket-employees-so-loyal-to-artie-t

Thompson, Derek. "The Economic History of the Last 2000 Years: Part II." *The Atlantic*. June 20, 2012. www.theatlantic.com/business/archive/2012/06/the-economic-history-of-the-last-2000-years-part-ii/258762/

Thunberg, Greta. *The Climate Book*. New York: Penguin, 2023.

Tosti-Kharas, Jennifer, Eric Lamm, and Tom E. Thomas. "Organization OR Environment? Disentangling Employees' Rationales Behind Organizational Citizenship Behavior for the Environment." *Organization & Environment* 30, no. 3 (2017): 187–210. https://doi.org/10.1177/1086026616668381

6   Meaningful Work and Society
What Will We Protect?

9/11 and the Role of Work in Society

The buildings that were destroyed in the September 11, 2001 terrorist attacks were so large that they were described as "a city within a city" by American Studies scholar Angus Gillespie in a "biography" of the original World Trade Center (WTC) that was published shortly before its demise. Most people associate the WTC with iconic photographs of two "cigarette boxes" that once towered over Lower Manhattan, literally poking holes, on some days, through the clouds, the same two burning skyscrapers that collapsed on 9/11. However, the WTC was actually a complex of seven buildings occupying a 16-acre "superblock" that, when it was built, disrupted the original traffic flow of three east-west streets and two north-south thoroughfares to make way for a massive plaza at the foot of the Twin Towers. It was estimated that 50,000 tenants and visitors occupied the buildings each workday, with many thousand more coursing through the subway and PATH train tunnels beneath the site that served as a transportation hub for commuters. The complex had its own postal code and police force and provided office space for private sector companies and state employees, a command center for city leadership, retail space below ground level, parking garages further down, and a hotel. Other office buildings and residential apartments surrounded the site. If we wish to understand the meaning and purpose of work as it relates to human community, the World Trade Center is a useful site to study the life, death, and rebirth of a society.

When Gillespie describes the "daily drudgery" of passengers disembarking from trains at the WTC, it is not clear whether he is referring to their commute, their workday ahead, or both. Once some of them made it into the lobby of one of the Twin Towers, they would be whisked upward by one of 254 elevators serving a complex system of "skylobbies" – like transfer portals – because each 110-story tower consisted, pragmatically speaking, of "three skyscrapers, stacked one on top of another." Once they reached their destination floors from those elevators, office workers would find their assigned corner offices or cramped cubicles where they would station themselves for most of the workday buying and selling bonds, trading

DOI: 10.4324/9781003307327-6

stocks, typing memos, answering telephones, and doing many other desk jobs needing to be performed inside as the buildings swayed almost imperceptibly while the wind blew outside, as designed. In the morning, coffee and newspaper vendors stood ready to supply them with the day's necessities, and in the afternoon, retail shops stayed open to enable them to shop for clothing, books, and headache remedies. Throughout the day and evening, kitchen staff, sommeliers, and servers at Windows on the World at the top of the North tower kept busy providing an experience for corporate events and romantic couples who wanted to see and be seen at "one of the highest-grossing restaurants in the world." Other restaurants hosted power lunches, while corporate cafeterias offered convenience, and delis delivered food throughout the system to stockbrokers who risked losing money if they left the trading floor even for a few minutes. An ecosystem of shoe shiners, dry cleaners, and personal assistants subsisted on those same trading floors and offices, trying to blend into the background behind the frenetic activity in the foreground. When most of the workers went home at the end of the workday, the nightlife would kick in at places like the Tall Ships Bar, where the suits unwound and may have been propositioned by sex workers or solicited by panhandlers. Even overnight, operations staff were ever-present in the towers, ensuring that the elevators were operating safely, maintaining heating and cooling systems, guarding expensive equipment, patrolling corridors, washing windows, and cleaning, among other services. The range of occupations represented in the WTC alone rivaled that of any city, as did the degree of economic inequality. Like other cities, the WTC required an infrastructure to make the rest of the work that took place there possible.

As James Glanz and Eric Lipton suggest in their post-9/11 book, *City in the Sky*, it is something of a miracle that the casualties were not greater when terrorists parked a Ford Econoline van full of dynamite in the parking garage beneath the hotel and North Tower on February 26, 1993. More than 1,000 people who descended darkened, hazy stairwells from their places of work suffered smoke inhalation, but the six victims who died either worked below ground or were near the parking garage at the time of the explosion. Gillespie suggests that the victim count would almost certainly have been higher had the terrorists parked the van near any other crowded space in the city but that they chose the WTC for its "symbolic significance." However, the impact of these attacks on work in the WTC was more than symbolic. He observes that Windows on the World shut down for several weeks and lost money that year. Meanwhile, in *On Top of the World*, Tom Barbash recalls that, even though none of the victims in 1993 were employees of bond broker Cantor Fitzgerald, the firm lost business because it did not have backup systems to access all the records and papers from which it was exiled while officials cleaned the buildings and engineers ensured their structural integrity. In a pre-Internet age, the firm could not do some of its work when it was out of the office.

That lesson would prove critical to Cantor's survival after 9/11. The firm lost 658 of 960 New York personnel – the most casualties of any single organization – and yet this time, it was ready for work when the bond markets reopened on the morning of September 13. The work was made possible, in part, by a disaster recovery site across the Hudson River in Rochelle Park, New Jersey, which had been set up in the event of another attack or other catastrophe. Meanwhile, Cantor had become a business leader in a move toward electronic bond trading – a disruptive development for an industry that had historically transacted with handshakes. Even as the firm's screens filled up with trades two days after the attacks, Richard Grasso, the chief executive of the New York Stock Exchange – the center of the equity trading world at the time – was sleeping in his office to supervise the cleanup of the physical trading floor without which stock trading would not resume until the following Monday. The Fire Department of New York lost 343 of its own on 9/11 – the second largest organizational loss after Cantor. The first responders were deployed from all over the city and surrounding areas to the site, "running toward danger," as the title of a book by the Newseum characterized their heroism. They came from every neighborhood of New York City, on duty, off duty, and on vacation, to fulfill the "fireman's oath" to selflessly serve. Stories of civilian heroism also became part of the 9/11 lore, including Prem Nath Jerash and Abe Zelmanowitz who were said to have stayed behind to comfort colleagues who could not navigate the stairways. Firefighters and other first responders figured heavily into "unbuilding the World Trade Center," the title of the first part of William Langewiesche's study, *American Ground*.

Thus, the workforces serving and supported by society changed with the circumstances: from the relative normalcy of a Wall Street ecosystem before 1993 and between the attacks of 1993 and 2001 to the crisis management and adaptation in the attacks' disruption and destruction to the unbuilding of the complex to the rebuilding and continuing the operation of the financial system that remains the predominant economic force in Lower Manhattan. A public dialogue among New Yorkers, prioritizing the voices of victims' families, determined that the city would build back even higher in the form of a new One World Trade Center building in support of a president's edict to remain "open for business" and in defiance of the terrorists' attempt to cut down America's "way of life." As chronicled in Philip Nobel's book, *Sixteen Acres*, the site was embroiled in political and aesthetic rancor about whose architect – the Lower Manhattan Development Corporation's or the leaseholder's – was responsible for designing the centerpiece of the master plan. Meanwhile, the footprints of the Twin Towers would remain "hallowed ground" and became a watery void around which a memorial was made bearing the names of all victims above two reflecting pools. Resolved to make Lower Manhattan more than a cemetery, the 9/11 Museum was situated partially below ground underneath the reflecting pools, cultural institutions were invited to submit proposals to occupy a performing arts space, a showy transportation hub was designed by Santiago Calatrava housing a shopping mall, and plans for an Islamic Community Center were on-again, off-again amid concern that the intention to support interfaith relations might embolden the kinds of extremists who carried out the attacks. The entire complex was outfitted with the most sophisticated post-9/11 security features, including constant monitoring, permanent barriers, and blast-proof glass, evidence of the work required to serve the evolving needs of society so that society can perform the work that is needed.

COVID-19 and the Role of Work in Society

On March 19, 2020, Christopher C. Krebs, Director of the Cybersecurity and Infrastructure Security Agency (CISA) of the United States Department of Homeland Security (DHS), issued a "Memorandum on Identification of Essential Critical Infrastructure Workers During COVID-19 Response." Deciphering that meandering title, it is apparent that the purpose of the memorandum was to provide guidance during the COVID-19 pandemic on who was to be considered an "essential critical infrastructure worker." Needless to say, at face value, it makes for dull reading. However, as any scholar of literature can attest, reading a text with a literary critical eye can reveal intriguing information about the intentions, interpretations, and situations of the author, the reader, and the world around them. From this perspective, to any reader of this memorandum that was not designed to be read as literature, there are several features of it that are curiously interesting.

One is that, unlike most memoranda that begin with a "To" field, there is no addressee. Beneath the date and title of the memorandum is Krebs' name, title, and affiliation, but as far as formal indicators go, the words that follow could well be written to anybody – or nobody in particular. Certainly, the average citizen was unlikely to read it, even though it could be obtained easily from the CISA website. But what concern did the average citizen have for cybersecurity and infrastructure security? These are the kinds of things that people take for granted that their government takes care of for them without giving them a second thought.

Read further, however, and you will find that the memorandum, clearly not intended only for CISA employees who worked for the Federal government in an agency of a department that had been created after the 9/11 attacks, revealed a lack of effective communication between other departments and agencies of the government that could potentially have prevented or mitigated the attacks. The memorandum says that state and local officials should use the guidance therein for implementation purposes.

However, neither was the memorandum exclusively directed at government officials – Federal, state, or local. It quotes the president's directive that, "If you work in a critical infrastructure industry, as defined by the Department of Homeland Security, such as healthcare services and pharmaceutical and food supply, you have a special responsibility to maintain your normal work schedule." The government might regulate the provision of healthcare services and pharmaceutical and food supply, but for the most part, people who work in those fields worked in the private sector. So perhaps it was written for them, too.

Further, although the memorandum – which was on CISA letterhead, complete with an official-looking seal – has the appearance of an imposing and authoritative directive from an obscure but important-sounding government agency, exactly one sentence in the two-page memorandum (plus appendices) is rendered in **bold text,** suggesting that, if the reader were rushing to perform critical infrastructure work and had no time to read the memo in its entirety, the bold sentence might be the *only* sentence they read: "**Accordingly, this list is advisory in nature. It is not, nor should it be considered to be, a federal directive or standard in and of itself.**" This is hardly a useful main point of the memorandum. Moreover, it seems to say, in other words, to read this memorandum with a grain of salt. As though to justify that grain of salt, in the months that followed, the memorandum would be updated several times as the world learned more about COVID-19.

CISA's list was summarized in the figure that follows that, for no stated reason, somewhat resembles a honeycomb, which might induce the critical reader to wonder whether a "busy bee" analogy was meant to be implied:

Figure 6.1 Essential Critical Infrastructure Workers

The list reinforces the sense that – even if it comes from a government agency and the wordy description "essential critical infrastructure workers" may seem to invoke a small number of government employees – the memorandum was aimed at advising, guiding, and encouraging, though not mandating, the continuation of innumerable types of work. However, unlike

after 9/11, when the president exhorted *everyone* to return to work to promote economic activity and as a show of defiance against terrorism, the CISA
COVID-19 memorandum did not tell *everyone* to get back to work. Outside
of these 16 hexagons were even more industries and occupations that were
not considered to be essential to the critical infrastructure.

What, for that matter, the critical reader might wonder, is a critical infrastructure, anyway? One can glean from the memorandum and its authoring
agency that a critical infrastructure consists primarily of technological and
physical features of society that, if disrupted, would lead to the collapse of
other features of society that depend upon them – and ultimately, perhaps,
to the collapse of society itself. For example, transportation – a critical infrastructure industry – is necessary to get employees of nuclear reactors – another
such industry – to work. If nuclear reactors were understaffed, they might be
vulnerable to actual meltdowns, which could lead to other figurative societal
meltdowns. To be sure, in a violent world, society needs defense – another industry on the diagram – in case there are nefarious actors attempting to take
down our nuclear reactors, dams, and commercial facilities. We need financial institutions so that we can have access to money to transport us to our
jobs where we make food and clean water, and we need emergency services
in case anyone gets hurt on or off the job. This is not necessarily to say we
do not need education, entertainment, and management consulting – among
other industries that are not part of the critical societal beehive – but perhaps
they are merely parasites upon the critical infrastructure foundations essential to the continuation of basic services necessary to survival.

If anything, the CISA memorandum urges us to recognize the essential
meaning and purpose of some work to societal survival and well-being. At
the same time, it may lead us to wonder which work is less essential and
whether it therefore has lesser or simply different significance to our chances
to live meaningful, purposeful lives.

Some work that was not deemed essential in Director Krebs' memorandum nonetheless seemed essential to those who performed it. Hundreds of
bar owners in Texas, whose establishments were not among the food venues
that were allowed to reopen under state law a few months after the initial
societal shutdown, began serving pre-packaged foods like chips and salsa so
that they could reclassify themselves as restaurants. Some belligerent owners
rationalized not only that it was essential for them to make a living for themselves but also to provide the essential service of a gathering place for their
patrons. Some such establishments even relied upon the uncivil disobedience
of armed anti-government protestors who purported to protect them from
anyone who sought to close their doors.

At the same time that such spuriously essential activities were being
treated as though they were indispensable, other essential societal functions
did not make authorities' lists of essential work. One was our own world of
higher education where, during what most institutions in the northern hemi-
sphere knew as Spring term 2020, students were sent home to pivot from

traditional, face-to-face classroom gatherings to online learning. Over the next several months, during what many of these institutions were grateful to have as a summer break, *The Chronicle of Higher Education* kept a log of thousands of institutions' return plans for the Fall term. Some prognosticators forecasted the end of the industry as we knew it, predicting that the efficacy of online learning would lead students around the globe to partake of a disruptive distance learning model offered by partnerships between a few elite universities and fewer elite technology companies.

The distinction between essential and inessential work was neither a bright line nor purely in the eye of the beholder. Perhaps a better way to explain what led some seemingly mundane work to be classified as essential and other seemingly significant work to be classified as inessential is to appeal to the so-called "Eisenhower Principle," often attributed to former United States President Dwight Eisenhower's method for prioritizing problems. He said, "I have two kinds of problems, the urgent and the important. The urgent are not important, and the important are never urgent." By this principle, maintaining the campus infrastructure to allow students to eat and sleep in college dorms was urgent, much as maintaining the critical infrastructure to allow healthcare workers to get to their hospitals was urgent. Meanwhile, continuing learning in virtual college classrooms was important but not urgent enough that it could not be postponed to allow instructors to figure out how to teach on Zoom, much as the return to face-to-face learning could wait until infection rates subsided.

Political and Economic Systems: From Shareholder to Stakeholder Capitalism

When we think about systems that govern our organizations and the individuals within them, two of the most important forces regulating work are the economic market and the political state. In many modern societies, these forces work together and in tension with each other and so are inseparable. The market is a system of economic organization that coordinates production – or what economists typically call "supply" – with consumption – or what economists typically call "demand" – that serves society's needs and wants. Theoretically, in a perfectly efficient market in which the flow of information is free and fair and each participant is a rational economic actor who is self-interested but does not wield excessive power, the so-called "invisible hand" of Adam Smith's ideal imagination would regulate supply with demand to yield a fair equilibrium price for goods and services. As most students of economics understand, the equilibrium price is the point at which the supply and demand curves intersect, meaning the supplier has sufficient economic motivation to produce a given quantity of a good or service that is demanded at that same price.

However, perfectly efficient markets do not exist in the real world. Information does not always flow freely and fairly, participants are not always rational, and power can be abused. Economists recognize several types of "market failures" that can disrupt the smooth operation of the invisible hand. They include natural monopolies, in which it is more efficient for one or two suppliers rather than many competitors to offer a good or service. During the pandemic, the United States government partnered with private industry in the race to develop, manufacture, and distribute a vaccine that would prevent or mitigate the spread of COVID-19. Although many companies joined the effort, the vaccination market in the United States was ultimately cornered by Pfizer and Moderna, who, together, as of this writing, had administered around 97% of total vaccines. Even though other vaccinations showed some promise and efficacy, the development and distribution costs were so high that after those two products had proven effective, it no longer made sense for the U.S. government or the other companies to sink additional investment into a monopolized market.

Another type of market failure concerns public goods, which are those to which consumers are perceived to have a moral right, regardless of their ability to pay. Again, the COVID-19 vaccination serves as a fitting example. There remains a debate within the United States' complex healthcare system about whether all citizens have an equal right to quality healthcare and ought to be required to purchase health insurance. However, the COVID-19 vaccine was made available, free of charge, to anyone for whom it was medically indicated on the premise that it was better for each citizen individually (to protect personal health) and for all citizens collectively (to protect public health) – even though vaccine skepticism and other forces led only around 80% of eligible patients to get vaccinated.

The push by public health officials to increase vaccination rates was, in part, motivated by external effects – another market failure that economists use to describe the potential for some people to bear the costs of decisions made by other people. For example, in a fair market, if a person who chose to remain unvaccinated were to infect a person who chose to get vaccinated (vaccine efficacy was not 100%, meaning it was still possible to get infected even if vaccinated), the costs of the latter ought to be borne by the former. However, often such externalities, as they are also called, are impossible to track and enforce.

Citizens living in the pandemic also had to contend with a market failure referred to as information asymmetry, when one party to a transaction, often the seller, has more information about the good or service than the buyer, who is vulnerable to deception or misinformation. Thus did purveyors of certain snake oil remedies profiteer from selling spurious solutions that either had no health benefits or that even had dangerous or fatal consequences for patients who took them uniformed. In modern capitalist economies, the political state is usually the party that regulates acceptable behavior within the marketplace so that these market failures are not exploited or abused by powerful market actors. The state may do so by, for example, taking responsibility for vaccine approvals, regulating control over vaccine distribution, campaigning for the benefits of vaccination, and providing other public health education.

Of course, in recent centuries, there has been considerable debate about whether the free market – despite its flaws – is a better system for coordinating societal production with consumption than a so-called planned economy. Even in capitalist markets, there has been lively debate over the past several decades about whether the purpose of business organizations within the market is to maximize profits or to serve a multiplicity of stakeholders. The libertarian economics of the late 20th century, exemplified by Milton Friedman's claim that "the social responsibility of business is to increase its profits," have been challenged by "stakeholder capitalism" and a variety of related ideas and ideals for business activity. Thinkers from philosopher R. Edward Freeman to World Economic Forum founder Klaus Schwab have been credited with articulating stakeholder capitalism as a new alternative to shareholder value maximization. Instead of positioning profit as an end in itself, stakeholder capitalism positions it as a monetary reward for fulfilling the moral responsibility of business to serve society's needs and wants. This view is roughly aligned with emerging ideas like "conscious capitalism," embraced by Whole Foods founder John Mackey; "shared value" capitalism, set forth by strategy scholar Michael Porter; and "triple bottom line" accounting – the idea that business performance ought to be measured by a balanced triad of economic, environmental, and social performance, not financial metrics alone.

Pricing and Protecting Work for Societal Good

All these forces and functions converged in the form of the September 11 Victim Compensation Fund (VCF), illustrating the interplay of the market and state in determining what work is meaningful to society and how those systems function to put a *price* on work and their responsibility – and limitations upon their capacity – to *protect* workers. As explained in *What is Life Worth?*, a book by Kenneth R. Feinberg, who was appointed Special Master of the VCF, it was created only 11 days after the attacks as part of the Air Transportation Safety and System Stabilization Act. One pragmatic function of the VCF was to avoid class action litigation that could destabilize the airline industry, which would be likely to harm an already tenuous American economy as a whole. Claimants were required to sign away their right to sue the airlines for the failure of their security systems to prevent the attacks. The normative function of the VCF was to grant tax-free compensation to victims' families who had suffered such a sudden, unprecedented, and catastrophic loss – often of a primary income earner. While that moral purpose of the VCF may have been justifiable, the novel nature of the VCF raised questions about what kind of losses did and did not warrant government compensation, from deaths in military combat to civilian casualties in other terrorist attacks, natural disasters, and infrastructure failures.

Feinberg did not purport to answer those questions but was aware that the mere existence of the VCF raised them. Rather, the kinds of questions that he had to answer included, but were not limited to, the pragmatic function of the market to *price* work and the normative function of the state to *protect* workers. With regard to the latter, one question that he had to consider was "Who was eligible to receive compensation?" At first, VCF compensation was restricted to families of those who died or were injured on 9/11. This, in turn, was complicated by who was considered to be a family member. For example, many victims were engaged to be married. Some involved a ring and a wedding date, neither of which constituted a legal contract but functioned as demonstrated evidence of intent. Others were moving in that direction but were not "official." Still others – such as same-sex partners – were not yet eligible for familial status in the laws of the day. According to an interview that Christopher conducted with Jackie Zins, one of Feinberg's senior staff members, and Stacy Pervall, a former PwC colleague of Christopher who managed a team of accountants supporting Feinberg's staff, one of the responsibilities of VCF representatives was to verify claims eligibility. What this grim task amounted to in practice was that those claiming to be family sometimes brought in boxes of personal mementos attesting to their relationships. Fraud was possible, though not rampant. Unfortunately, intra-family disputes also transpired, for example, between birth families and betrothed. All of this is to suggest that the function of the state to protect workers was inseparable from the state's – or in this case, the VCF's, as an operative of the state – determination of what kinds of relationships ought to be seen as beneficiaries of the victim's work and loss of their ability to provide.

The restrictions on compensation eligibility also resulted in the denial of the claim of Mariane Pearl, the wife of *Wall Street Journal* reporter Danny Pearl, who was kidnapped and beheaded in Pakistan a few months after the attacks by religious extremists believed to be aligned with the perpetrators of the 9/11 attacks. In her book, *A Mighty Heart*, Mariane Pearl describes the dangerous work of a journalist investigating terrorism and meeting with a clandestine network of contacts in search of answers. She does not set forth conclusions about whose responsibility it ultimately is to protect the life of a journalist any more than it is clear that her husband was or was not a victim of the same forces that claimed the lives of 9/11 victims. Other claimants to the VCF whose status was initially uncertain were those who came to believe that chronic illnesses and cancer diagnoses might have been related to the inhalation of toxic fumes atop the pile during the rescue and recovery ("unbuilding") effort. Indeed, research backs that World Trade Center responders and survivors do have increased cancer risks compared to the general population – an effect that may last for decades to come. More than 20 years later, claimants continue to come forward as acts of Congress have, sometimes contentiously, extended the operation of the VCF.

With regard to the pragmatic function of the market to price work, Feinberg considered the questions, "How much money should be awarded? What rationale should govern the awards?" alongside the titular question of what life is worth in his book. Broadly speaking, Feinberg first had to consider whether each life should be valued equally – as they are said to be created in the American Constitution – or whether their unequal market value should usurp equality when it came to compensating victims' families for not only the loss of a loved one but also the loss of their work-related income. In his book, Feinberg describes his sympathy for some families of the poorest workers at the WTC, including that of Ivhan Luis, a line cook preparing to go to college who earned less than US$20,000 in 2000 and 2001 combined. Meanwhile, he betrays some frustration with representatives of the richest, such as representatives of Cantor Fitzgerald victims who did not want their families – some of which were accustomed to living on incomes well over US$1 million a year – to be short-changed. The formula for determining awards that Feinberg ultimately used probably had less to do with what life is truly worth in the big picture than its price in the marketplace. The factors that influenced the unequal size of the awards included the victim's earning history, age, and expected future earnings had they not died, along with other factors such as dependents and the family's ability to maintain its standard of living in the wake of loss. The formula did not, however, account for the value of the victim's work to society – for example, in the form of a bonus for the heroism of the first responders who willingly risked their lives to save others for which some stakeholders advocated. A rudimentary analysis of VCF awards suggests that first responders' families received, on average, around US$1 million less than those of financiers. There was a minimum award, and the formula limited the maximum size of an award for the very top income earners, but beyond those considerations at the extremes, the VCF for the most part relied on the pragmatic function of the market to price the value of work.

Whereas the primary role of the VCF was, indirectly, to compensate families for income lost due to the death or injury of a loved one, a series of loosely coordinated employer, employee, and government practices emerged in the COVID-19 pandemic directly to compensate workers themselves – and those dependent upon them – for the performance of risky essential work and loss of employment. Workers at a meatpacking plant where the infection was difficult to contain were incentivized to show up to work for a cash "responsibility bonus," while cashiers, personal shoppers, and shelf stockers at retail establishments were sometimes rewarded with "hazard pay." On one hand, such payment practices were a natural response to market norms in which a lower supply of willing and able workers amid growing demand led to higher equilibrium prices for their labor, but they might also be taken as a signal that the perception of the normative value of essential work increases during times of duress. But the market could not correct for a net loss of jobs other than to pass and then extend legislation to provide unemployment compensation. One unintended consequence of the government's action to *protect* workers was that it interfered with the market's capacity to *price* work in a way that would motivate some workers – who stood to make as much or more money by remaining unemployed – to get back to work when it was safe and possible to do so. But such extraordinary circumstances were temporary. When the public health emergency had relented and some employees had the leverage to decide what kind of working conditions they wished to return to, a vast reshuffling of the labor market that some called The Great Resignation contributed once again to price instability, especially for less desirable but necessary jobs.

Perhaps, in a perfect efficient market, the value of work as expressed in its price/wage would be commensurate with its value to society. The stories of both 9/11 and the pandemic are full of work that was valuable to society – from first responders to frontline workers – that were not only among the lowest price work classifications but also among the least protected. Whether this is a general truth or a particular idiosyncrasy of the market is probably less important than the fact that any of us may be faced with the choice, at some point in our work lives, between doing self-interested work for better pay and doing more socially valuable work for less money. This tension is similar or even perhaps the same as that between pursuing work for pay or chasing a calling for a higher purpose that may pay less. As we have seen, Wrzesniewski and colleagues defined callings as "personally fulfilling or socially valuable," setting off significant debate among calling scholars between whether a calling must be one, the other, or both, which raises a normative question, whether we *ought to* pursue work for personal fulfillment, whether that comes in the form of meaning or money, or social value. Which one should we choose?

The preferred answer, of course, is both. Organizational psychologist Adam Grant refers to the real phenomenon of being driven to do socially beneficial work as "prosocial motivation," while philosopher Norman Care says we ideally should seek self-realization in those work activities that serve others. As our 9/11 and pandemic research demonstrates, many first responders and frontline workers did not see their work as a sacrifice at all. To the contrary, they found personal fulfillment not only in serving others but also working alongside like-minded people. For every *New York Times* portrait or profile of a victim who was characterized as a selfless hero, there was another Portrait of a victim who – neither selflessly nor selfishly – happened to relish the camaraderie of colleagues. There were still others who were depicted as working for the material benefits of early retirement and a lifetime pension. In reality, for many people in socially valuable professions, all these forces coexisted in their decision to stay in their chosen profession. It would be wonderful if we did not have to choose between personal fulfillment and social value, but Care concludes that, if we were forced to do so, we are obligated, in an imperfect world that needs us to work, to choose to serve others.

Questions and Prompts for Review and Reflection About Chapter 6

- Is it fair that society often pays the least for work that is the most valuable to its functioning?
- Should people in general prioritize personal fulfillment or societal benefits in the search for work? Why?
- How do you personally think about the tradeoff between societal value and income in your own work choices, now and over the course of your career?
- How could our economic and political systems, through public policy, be changed to help compensate those whose work society does not sufficiently recognize?
- How can we, as a society, think about protecting work that performs a social good?

Chapter 6 References

Barbash, Tom. *On Top of the World: Cantor Fitzgerald, Howard Lutnick, and 9/11: A Story of Loss and Renewal*. New York: Harper, 2003.

Bush, George W. "Statement by the President in His Address to the Nation." *The White House Web Archive*. September 11, 2001. https://georgewbush-whitehouse. archives.gov/news/releases/2001/09/20010911-16.html

Care, Norman S. "Career Choice." *Ethics* 94, no. 2 (1984): 283–302.

The Chronicle of Higher Education. "Here's Our List of Colleges' Reopening Models." Accessed February 26, 2024. www.chronicle.com/article/heres-a-list-of-colleges-plans-for-reopening-in-the-fall/

Eisenhower, Dwight D. "Address at the Second Assembly of the World Council of Churches, Evanston, Illinois." *The American Presidency Project*. August 19, 1954. https://web.archive.org/web/20150402111315/www.presidency.ucsb.edu/ws/?pid=9991

Elkind, Peter. "The Fall of the House of Grasso." *Fortune*. October 18, 2004. https://money.cnn.com/magazines/fortune/fortune_archive/2004/10/18/8188087/index.htm

Elkington, John. "Enter the Triple Bottom Line." In *The Triple Bottom Line: Does It All Add Up?*, edited by Adrian Henriques and Julie Richardson, 1–16. Routledge, 2004. https://doi.org/10.4324/9781849773348

Feinberg, Kenneth R. *What Is Life Worth? The Unprecedented Effort to Compensate the Victims of 9/11*. New York: PublicAffairs, 2006.

Fernandez, Manny, and David Montgomery. "Businesses Chafing Under Covid-19 Lockdowns Turn to Armed Defiance." *The New York Times*. May 13, 2020. www.nytimes.com/2020/05/13/us/coronavirus-businesses-lockdown-guns.html

Gillespie, Angus K. *Twin Towers: The Life of New York City's Trade Center*. New York: NAL Trade, 2002.

Glanz, James, and Eric Lipton. *City in the Sky: The Rise and Fall of the World Trade Center*. New York: Times Books, 2003.

Grant, Adam M., and Justin M. Berg. "Prosocial Motivation at Work: When, Why, and How Making a Difference Makes a Difference." In *The Oxford Handbook of Positive Organizational Scholarship*, edited by Kim Cameron and Gretchen Spreitzer, 28–44. Oxford: Oxford University Press, 2012.

Jones, Calley. "The Toll of Heroism: Increased Cancer Incidence Among 9/11 Responders." *American Association for Cancer Research*. September 9, 2022. www.aacr.org/blog/2022/09/09/the-toll-of-heroism-increased-cancer-incidence-among-9-11-responders/

Kinder, Molly, Laura Stateler, and Julia Du. "Windfall Profits and Deadly Risks: How the Biggest Retail Companies Are Compensating Essential Workers During the COVID-19 Pandemic." *Brookings*. November 2020. www.brookings.edu/articles/windfall-profits-and-deadly-risks/

Krebs, Christopher C. "Memorandum on Identification of Essential Critical Infrastructure Workers During COVID-19 Response." *United States Department of Homeland Security, Cybersecurity and Infrastructure Security Agency*. March 19, 2020. www.cisa.gov/sites/default/files/publications/CISA-Guidance-on-Essential-Critical-Infrastructure-Workers-1-20-508c.pdf

Langewiesche, William. "American Ground: Unbuilding the World Trade Center." *The Atlantic*. July/August 2002. www.theatlantic.com/magazine/archive/2002/07/excerpts-from-american-ground-unbuilding-the-world-trade-center/302542/

Levin, Tim. "Education Is More Ripe for Disruption Than Nearly Any Other Industry, Says NYU Professor Scott Galloway: 'Harvard Is Now a $50,000 Streaming Platform'." *Business Insider*. December 9, 2020. www.businessinsider.com/nyu-professor-scott-galloway-college-access-equity-future-education-disruption-2020-12

Lussenhop, Jessica. "Coronavirus at Smithfield Pork Plant: The Untold Story of America's Biggest Outbreak." *BBC News*. April 17, 2020. www.bbc.com/news/world-us-canada-52311877

Mackey, John, and Raj Sisodia. *Conscious Capitalism*. Boston, MA: Harvard Business Review Press, 2014.

Michaelson, Christopher. "Twenty Years After 9/11 Part Three: A Conversation with Jackie Zins & Stacy Pervall, Former Representatives of the 9/11 Victim Compensation Fund." *Work in Progress*. August 30, 2021. www.buzzsprout.com/175109 6/9109769-twenty-years-after-9-11-part-three-a-conversation-with-jackie-zins-stacy-pervall-former-representatives-of-the-9-11-victim-compensation-fund

Mikulic, Matej. "COVID-19 Vaccinations Administered in the U.S. as of April 2023, by Manufacturer." *Statista*. Accessed February 26, 2024. www.statista.com/statistics/1198516/covid-19-vaccinations-administered-us-by-company/

Newseum. *Running Toward Danger: Stories Behind the Breaking News of September 11*. Lanham, MD: Rowman & Littlefield, 2002.

The New York Times. "Portraits of Grief." Accessed September 11, 2023. https://archive.nytimes.com/www.nytimes.com/interactive/us/sept-11-reckoning/portraits-of-grief.html

Nobel, Philip. *Sixteen Acres: Architecture and the Outrageous Struggle for the Future of Ground Zero*. New York: Metropolitan Books, 2005.

Pearl, Mariane. *A Mighty Heart: The Inside Story of the Al Qaeda Kidnapping of Danny Pearl*. New York: Scribner, 2004.

Phillips, James, Jordan Selzer, Samantha Noll, and Timur Alptunaer. "Covid-19 Has Closed Stores, But Snake Oil Is Still for Sale." *The New York Times*. March 31, 2020. www.nytimes.com/2020/03/31/opinion/fake-treatment-cure-coronavirus.html

Porter, Michael E., and Mark R. Kramer. "Creating Shared Value." *Harvard Business Review*. January-February 2011. https://hbr.org/2011/01/the-big-idea-creating-shared-value

Rohrer, Finlo. "The Battle Over the 'Ground Zero Mosque'." *BBC News*. August 3, 2010. www.bbc.com/news/world-us-canada-10846716

Russell, Ben. "Hundreds of Texas Bars Have Reopened as 'Restaurants'." *NBC DFW*. September 17, 2020. www.nbcdfw.com/news/local/hundreds-of-texas-bars-have-reopened-as-restaurants/2445456/

September 11th Victim Compensation Fund. "2023 Annual Report." Accessed February 27, 2024. www.vcf.gov/

7 The Future of Meaningful Work

A Framework for a Purpose-Driven Era

A Tale of Meaning and Purpose

Early on in this book, we told the story of how 9/11, which we thought would be the defining catastrophe of our lifetimes, prompted us and many others to reflect on meaning and purpose and influenced our career changes from management consulting to academia. Almost 20 years later, another catastrophe – vastly different in provenance, timeline, and scale from the first, each tragic in its own way – led us and others to contemplate meaning and purpose again. Both events were inseparable from the working world in terms of both their impact and responses to them, and if any good can come from adversity, they taught us invaluable lessons about what work means in our lives and why we ought to work for a purpose that matters.

As Charles Dickens might have put it if he had written a tale of two tragedies that transformed work in the 21st century: It was the most extraordinary of times; it was the most ordinary of times. The changes in the world of work as we lived through them seemed singular to us and yet were no different than the evolution of the workplace in any period of history. It was the age of "do what you love"; it was the age of "work 'til you die" – but this tension between possibility and necessity was present in any age. It was the era of coworking; it was the era of the virtual workplace – much as the concept of "telecommuting" to the office had once seemed novel. It was the season of overwork; it was the season of underemployment – themes for all seasons. It was the spring of voluntary resignation; it was the winter of involuntary unretirement – history repeating itself once again. It was the time of the self-made billionaire; it was the time of income inequality – a gap between haves and have-nots that more often waxed than waned. It was time for the future of work to arrive; the future of work was always in the future.

The fact that these questions and considerations had appeared in other times did not mean they were any less important to the people confronting them in these times. Workers wondered whether their work was worth the sacrifices it demanded of them, reflecting upon whether they had a purpose in life to point them toward a calling at work or considering the prospect of work that made a more meaningful contribution to the world than the work

DOI: 10.4324/9781003307327-7

they had been trained to perform. It was the epoch in which there was no end of work to be done; it was the epoch in which futurists foresaw the end of work altogether – a century after economist John Maynard Keynes predicted 3-hour shifts and a 15-hour work week.

The pandemic coincided with – and arguably accelerated – technology adoption that the organizers of the world's most important power meeting (the World Economic Forum Annual Meeting in Davos, Switzerland) proclaimed to be a "Fourth Industrial Revolution." A year after the post-IPO crash a coworking giant with a charismatic founder who professed the social and economic benefits of shared workspace (WeWork), a video-telephony firm that few had heard of became the ubiquitous noise of the remote workplace (Zoom). While office workers were enabled by technology to work from anywhere, some frontline workers could not find work anywhere after being put out of work by primitive robots. Those who were forced into unemployment could hardly afford to live. At the same time, a contingent of workers who thought their lives were worth more than to be wasted doing the work they were doing spawned a Great Resignation, affording them the freedom to reclaim passions worth living for.

According to the most optimistic among the Fourth Industrial Revolutionaries, the good news for the problem of meaningless work was that the end of work was nigh. Robots were already replacing manual laborers. Gradually, artificial intelligence would think for us, too. Political philosopher John Rawls and political economist Philippe Van Parijs disagreed about whether, if the machines did all the work for us, Malibu surfers would deserve to be paid Universal Basic Incomes.

However, the pessimists shared the bad news that the problems with waiting for the end of work to find our purpose included, for one thing, unemployment, and for another, nobody knew how long we would have to keep working before we were set free. After all, it had been nearly a full century since Keynes made his premature prediction that "technological unemployment" would soon render work unnecessary. The end of work would, in turn, make the question of the meaning and purpose of work obsolete.

Perhaps rumors of the death of work had been greatly exaggerated. We look with optimism toward a future of work in which the most deleterious tasks are performed by technology, the most enlivening responsibilities still belong to humans, and we all work a little bit less, with greater options and opportunities and more attention to work that supports meaning and purpose in our lives. In the meantime, we remain cautious about the transition to that future of work, during which those who can least afford to lose their work may be the most vulnerable to technological unemployment.

As Dickens might have imagined, "all these things, and a thousand like them, came to pass in and close upon" us in these uncertain times that were no more uncertain and no less certain than other times. They commanded us to prepare, at the same time, to find meaning and purpose amid the future of work and within a world without work, whichever came to pass.

The Future of Meaningful Work

While we were writing this book, we were also putting the finishing touches on the introduction to a 2023 special issue of the *Journal of Business Ethics*, one of the premiere peer-reviewed academic journals on business ethics. Our issue was titled, "Ethics and the Future of Meaningful Work," which we co-guest-edited with our colleagues Evgenia Lysova, Luke Fletcher, Catherine Bailey, and Peter McGhee. In our research for this article, we found that speculation about the future of work proceeds along several dimensions: political-institutional, social-demographic, economic, and technological. As its name suggests, the political-institutional dimension is broad, encompassing the market for labor and relationships between the state, organizations' license to operate within the state, and individuals' employment within those organizations. In short, the *political-institutional* dimension of the future of work is about questions that focus on *what*: If there is human work in the future, what work will there be?

The World Economic Forum's annual report on the Future of Jobs suggests that, although the future is not yet here, the workforce of today must prepare for the workplace of tomorrow. That message, some variation on which has been the focus of the report since the Forum's founder Klaus Schwab coined the term "Fourth Industrial Revolution" in 2016, is likely to persist into a foreseeable future in which human beings will learn to adapt to new ways of working augmented by emerging technologies and demands. As two leaders of Jen's former firm explain in their 2018 book *Human + Machine*, that language of augmentation of human work by technology is more promising and less intimidating than the prospect of machines taking away work from people without creating new, reskilled, and upskilled human employment opportunities. Even as we were writing this book, the latest job update at the World Economic Forum's annual meeting reported, unsurprisingly, that some of the top skills needed in the marketplace of the present involved technological literacy. However, at the top of the list were skills like analysis, creativity, and even curiosity and empathy, that were distinctly human capabilities.

The political-institutional dimension of the future of work is closely related to the *economic* dimension, which, unsurprisingly, governs questions of *quantity*: *How* much, for how much money, and *when* should we work? Somewhere in between a future full of work and a future bereft of work is a likely future with less work than the world we currently live in. Although there is little debate about the productivity benefits of industrialization, our demands and expectations over time for greater productivity and variety have meant that the effect on the supply of labor required have not been as significant as should otherwise be expected. Studies suggest that modern workers clock fewer hours per year than early industrial workers and pre-industrial workers, but the decline has not been consistent, and there is significant variance across markets. Moreover, the overall decline in input of labor hours over time has not been as dramatic as the increase in productivity output. The globalization of the economy along with the ubiquity of communications technologies mean that, although the quantity of hours we work today may be less than yesterday, the intensity of those hours may be greater. In other words, we work less than people used to but we still work harder and not as much less than we probably should.

The economic dimension of the future of work is also concerned with such matters as income inequality. As we have already noted, an overall increase in GDP per capita does not necessarily entail distributive justice when inequality is rising at an even greater rate than average wages. When wages lag behind inflation, to maintain their standard of living, workers have to work longer hours and/or postpone retirement. Meanwhile, as human life spans extend, working lives may also lengthen in order to fund longer lives and/or to keep them interesting.

In this way, the economic dimension of the future of work is integral to the social-demographic dimension, which concerns *who* works and how the evolution of work affects them and the opportunities available to them. As Anne Case and Angus Deaton observe in their book *Deaths of Despair*, even though the world at the end of the 20th century as a whole enjoyed "greater prosperity and greater longevity than at any time in history," the beginning of the 21st century has seen an increase in "deaths of despair," brought on by suicides, drug overdoses, and disease with economic, social, or psychological causes. Certainly, these concerns transcend the world of work, but they are also inseparable from the world of work that has the potential to affect life satisfaction by conferring or denying wages, providing or taking employment, and supporting or undermining the sense of meaning and purpose to which, as we have seen, work can add to or detract.

As with all of these dimensions of the future of work, the social-demographic dimension does not only portend bad news. As we have noted previously, the emerging generation of workers has been called the "purpose generation" because it has been dealt a difficult hand – environmental, economic, political, social, and technological risks as classified by the World Economic Forum's annual *Global Risk Report*. But this generation is also, arguably, informed and prepared to confront these challenges with purpose, passion, and technological acumen.

The fourth dimension of the future of work is often the first one we think of when we wonder and worry about the future of work and naturally influences all the other dimensions as well: the *technological* dimension, which influences *where* and *how* we work. It was technology that made it possible for the world to continue working when workplaces closed in the pandemic, and when they reopened after the public health emergency, it was still technology that held center stage in the ongoing conversation about whether remote employees could continue working from home. Moreover, as we have seen previously, it will continue to be technology that determines the changing ways in which we perform our work. Meanwhile, the evolution of artificial intelligence will decide whether those capabilities we previously characterized as especially human – including but not limited to analysis, creativity, curiosity, and empathy – are, indeed, uniquely so.

Not coincidentally, these dimensions of the future of work cover every one of the conventional journalistic questions – who, what, where, when, why, and how – that we ask in order to understand a project, phenomenon, or story, except the one most closely associated with meaning and purpose: why.

A '6 P' Framework of Functional and Moral Purposes of Work

Why do we work? The foregoing chapters of this book suggest that work and the meaning and management thereof takes place at three levels of analysis that typically inform the perspectives of management scholars. The individual, organizational, and systemic are called "nested" levels of analysis because individuals work within organizations and organizations operate within systems, and therefore, they are inseparable from one another. It is impossible to consider work at any level without understanding their interdependency with the other levels. Systems, ultimately, function to promote the welfare of individuals, bringing the three nested levels of analysis to a full circle.

We examined the individual level of analysis in Chapters 3 and 4 of this book, where we touched upon many attempts to explain why we work as individuals. The frameworks we explored share a broader and special reason we pursue work: that work – better than leisure, play, or other non-work endeavors – enables us to pursue those goals. In that sense, work, in general, is a means to the end of our individual, goal-oriented lives that cannot attain those goals without work.

Of course, because we ordinarily work in organizations – as examined in Chapter 5 – we are not free willy-nilly to pursue our own goals, irrespective of our responsibilities to the organization. Rather, we have a responsibility to perform the work that the organization asks of us in return for the employment that the organization has provided to us. In doing so, as we saw, we typically produce far more effectively and efficiently a collective effort than we would if we were each pursuing our separate goals individually.

In turn – as examined in Chapter 6 – the organizations produce those goods and services in the context of a market system that confers value upon our work by – as an Economics 101 student can attest – pricing our labor at the point of intersection between the supply and demand curves. In most such market systems, however, a political system regulates the market to correct for, as we have seen, market imperfections and other forces that can interfere with important priorities on which a price cannot easily be placed. Those include the right to employment opportunities, non-discrimination, and freedom from labor price exploitation that the government has responsibility to protect. This completes the circle of these three levels of analysis, in that the systemic protection of labor and human rights entails individual opportunity to pursue meaning and purpose at work.

The analytical framework that we have just outlined proposes six words, each felicitously beginning with the letter 'P,' that: Pursue and Perform (individual level), Provide and Produce (organization level), and Price and Protect (system level). Each of these '6 P's,' as we will refer to them (see the following table), can be used, conveniently, as a verb. We have placed the 6 P's in the levels where they conventionally occur, but they can potentially occur at the other levels, too. Within each level, one of the 6 P's has a primarily functional purpose – why we do it – whereas the other of the 6 P's at that level has a largely moral purpose – why we *ought to* do it, in a sense that implies something meaningful.

So, at the individual level of analysis, pursuing work is a functional activity. As Chapter 3 demonstrates, we think of the three work orientations – job, career, and calling – as reasons *why we work*. Wrzesniewski et al. describe the work orientations as relationships we have to our work, which has largely been taken by other researchers to explain what *meanings* our work may have to us – to review, as a means to pay (job), promotion (career), or passion (calling). While this implies that work orientations describe the relationship between an individual and a particular work role, it does not preclude us from thinking about how work orientations can motivate the *pursuit* of work that we may not (yet) possess. As we have seen, some people just want a job that they can do while they are working and forget about when they are not, whereas others hold out for a calling – and risk unemployment or unfulfillment until and unless they succeed. This situation suggests that work orientations are not just relationships between an individual and a role but that some people are inclined to certain work orientations in any role they seek. In this sense, work orientations may not merely be sources of meaning but also potential sources of work motivation – which may be especially palpable in the pursuit of progression to the next level of the career ladder.

Still at an individual level of analysis, after the successful pursuit of work leads to a secure position, we take on moral obligations – to ourselves and/or to others – to *perform* the work we have agreed to do. Whereas work orientations that we discussed in Chapter 3 focus on what we *get* out of work, many of the other frameworks that we introduced in Chapter 4 focus on both what we *get and give* through the work we do. So, for example, several frameworks prioritize mindful activity over mindless repetition – which is both good for our individual human development and likely to lead to better work performance – in the form of industrious input and quality output. For example, Arendt places action over labor much as Pence elevates craftsmanship above labor, while Bogan prefers doing to drifting. Other frameworks emphasize that the obligation to perform concerns our moral responsibilities to do work for the benefit of people including but not limited to ourselves. For example, Michaelson's normative conception of meaningful work asserts that what makes work meaningful is not merely what is subjectively pleasing to ourselves, and Care claims that we ought to choose service to others if it is in tension with self-realization.

While the responsibility of the individual worker to others was framed previously as a moral duty, there are also mutual contractual legal responsibilities between employees and their employers in a capitalist system in which work is the employee's property to sell to owners of capital. At the organizational level, *providing* work is a functional transaction between the employing organization and the employee. In policy debates, providing work is sometimes also framed as a moral responsibility toward job creation, though we would contend that the mere creation of jobs – if those jobs are not purposeful – is a pragmatic function and morally neutral. In that sense, organizational employers *provide* work opportunities, including a division of labor structure and the roles therein that individual employees *perform*. For example, although, in Chapter 5, we compare our former roles as management consultants to the deleterious work of pin factory workers, it also warrants repeating that, at the point in time that we had those positions, they were our dream jobs. We worked with talented colleagues for globally known brands and learned how to contribute to economic activity in ways we never could have done without the organizations that provided those opportunities to us.

It was only after a few years in those environments – and with the benefit of many more years of hindsight reflection – that we began to realize the ways in which operating in the leverage model was primarily a mechanism to maximize our ability as an organization to *produce*. In fact, production was so central to those organizations and the system in which they operated that profit – another 'P' – was seen as a reward for efficient production rather than a morally corrupting force. As much as our employer organizations and the individuals who supervised our work wanted us to stay motivated to perform by making grandiose claims about organizational purpose, their primary concern was less about the meaning we derived from our work and more about maximizing organizational production by attracting and retaining high-performing employees who got enough out of work – whatever their motivation – to keep giving. The situation is different in other types of organizations, like worker-owned B Corps, in which profit and purpose may be more aligned. All of these 'P's' – providing, profiting, and producing, among others – may have moral purposes, demonstrating the potentially blurry line between functional and moral purpose. In an ideally moral market, however, production of goods and services to supply the legitimate needs and wants of societal demand is the ultimate moral purpose toward which the provision of jobs is a means and of which profit is an earned consequence.

If we were perfectly rational economic actors in a perfectly efficient market, our functional motivation to work would be to earn the greatest *price* for our labor for the least amount of effort. However, most of us are not perfectly rational economic actors, nor, as we have seen, is our market perfectly efficient. We work to make a living, to be sure, but we also work toward other goods, including but not limited to goods like meaning and purpose, on which it may be impossible to place a reliable price. But, although individual workers may not always be rational economic actors, employers often are rational in their pursuit of the lowest-priced labor who can perform the work needed most efficiently. For much of the 20th century, globalization placed pricing pressures on what manual laborers could earn as employers sought to reduce manufacturing costs. In the 21st century, technological innovation has been the most significant price competition in both the manual and knowledge economies. These systemic forces have the potential to render obsolete the skills some people bring to the working world in exchange for a living, while opening up opportunities for them to "upskill" and "reskill" to adapt to a changing reality of work – or the possibility of no work.

The very fact that we are asking whether there will be work in the future suggests that – far-fetched or far away though that future may be – it is at least a useful thought experiment to imagine what kind of a world a world without work would be. Pessimistically, a world without work would be a boon for technology investors and a bust for everyone else whose job was replaced by technology. It would be a world of widening income inequality in which the fortunate few prospered and the unfortunate many competed for a shrinking pie of economically viable labor. The prospect of temporary or permanent unemployment brought about by systemic, technological forces beyond workers' control suggests that a moral purpose of the system that prices employment might be to *protect* workers from unjust prices, imperfect markets, and income inequality gone wild.

A more optimistic perspective on a world without work imagines the possibility that one of the government's protective functions would be to guarantee a Universal Basic Income to everyone. In such a scenario, technology would provide basic goods and services for human beings to enjoy in their ample leisure time. Some technology workaholics would still develop and invest in better technologies, perhaps enriching themselves in the process, but nobody would be deprived of the fundamentals to survive. Would such a society be, in aggregate, more prosperous? As individuals, would we flourish? What would you do with all of your free time if you never had to work and you had a disposable income to enjoy it?

Although UBI pilot tests, including a nationwide test in Finland in 2017–2018, have been perceived to be largely successful, we do not yet have reasons to believe that either the purely pessimistic or purely optimistic scenario about the future of work will become reality in the foreseeable future. The transition to a technologically autonomous future is likely to be long, complicated, and fraught with fears that artificial intelligence could usurp human intelligence in ways that could threaten human control over our future. Even a successful transition to a utopian, UBI-supported society is unlikely to end work altogether as individuals seek to supplement their meager minimum incomes. Rather, the future is still unfolding, and in the foreseeable future, there remains plenty of work to be done.

Table 7.1 Functional and Moral Work Purposes at Three Levels of Analysis (6 P's)

Level of Analysis	Individual	Organizational	Systemic
Functional Purpose (Why we do it)	*Pursue* work to serve a related goal	*Provide* work through job creation	*Price* labor in the free market
Moral Purpose (Why we ought to)	*Perform* work to fulfill responsibilities	*Produce* goods and services	*Protect* work and the rights of workers

Who, What, Where, When, How – and Why – to Work

As they prepare for this future of work, our students over the years have always asked who, what, where, when, and how. Their questions have included, for example:

- Who should my professional role models be? Who should be part of my professional network? Who should I work for – myself, my family, or my community? Who should I work for, in terms of an employer who shares my values?
- What industry should I enter? What skills do I need to succeed? What degrees and certifications will help me advance?
- Where or in what organization will I make the most money, learn the most, and be happiest? Where or in what city should I start my career? Where will my career take me?
- When should I leave this job for the next one? When should I go back to school? Start a family? When will I reach my professional goals? When can I retire?
- How should I ask for more pay and a promotion? How much money do I need to be happy? How should I protect my career from artificial intelligence who may be able to do what I do faster, better, and cheaper?

We empathize with all of these questions because they may be universal to anyone who has ever wondered about the meaning and purpose of their work, and so, we have asked them ourselves about our present careers as professors, just as we did about our past careers in management consulting. While we cannot possibly answer them for you – each person's experiences and preferences are uniquely their own – we hope this book has been helpful to your contemplation of these and similar questions. We would like, however, to share some of the kinds of thoughts that we offer our students on the final day of class, which usually is our last opportunity to confirm that they have taken away from our courses what we hoped they would learn.

Among all of these urgent and important questions that our students have asked – *Why?* – is, arguably, the most important, and yet, can feel the least urgent. It is the question in the back of the minds of the students we have ourselves been, encountered, and/or taught since the dawn of the new century, and yet it is rarely in the front of their minds – unless a tragedy forces it there. Rather, the kinds of questions about work that our students have asked us over the years have more often been pragmatic – what to do next in the foreseeable future – than normative – why to do it in the existential long-term. Ultimately, however, we see meaning and purpose at the roots of every question that our students are contemplating not only about the future of work, in general, but *their* future of work, in particular. You cannot answer who, what, when, where, and how to work without having a sense of why work matters to you, to the world, and in itself.

Chapter 7 References

AARP. "What Does Increasing Life Expectancy Mean for the Future of Work?" Accessed February 27, 2024. www.aarpinternational.org/initiatives/future-of-work/megatrends/longevity

Case, Anne, and Angus Deaton. *Deaths of Despair and the Future of Capitalism.* Princeton, NJ: Princeton University Press, 2020.

Daugherty, Paul H., and H. James Wilson. *Human + Machine: Reimagining Work in the Age of AI.* Boston, MA: Harvard Business Review Press, 2018.

Davidson, Adam. *The Passion Economy: The New Rules for Thriving in the Twenty-First Century.* New York: Alfred A. Knopf, 2020.

Dickens, Charles. *A Tale of Two Cities.* New York: Signet Classics, 1997.

Future of Life Institute. "Pause Giant AI Experiments: An Open Letter." Accessed February 27, 2024. https://futureoflife.org/open-letter/pause-giant-ai-experiments/

Giattino, Charlie, Esteban Ortiz-Ospina, and Max Roser. "Working Hours." *Our World in Data.* 2013. Accessed February 27, 2024. https://ourworldindata.org/working-hours

Green, Francis, Alan Felstead, Duncan Gallie, and Golo Henseke. "Working Still Harder." *ILR Review* 75, no. 2 (2022): 458–487. https://doi.org/10.1177/0019793920977850

Hitt, Michael A., Paul W. Beamish, Susan E. Jackson, and John E. Mathieu. "Building Theoretical and Empirical Bridges Across Levels." *Academy of Management Journal* 50, no. 6 (2007): 1385–1399. https://doi.org/10.5465/amj.2007.28166219

Hoover, Amanda. "The End of the Zoom Boom." *Wired.* February 8, 2023. www.wired.com/story/zoom-layoffs-future/

Hurst, Aaron. *The Purpose Economy: How Your Desire for Impact, Personal Growth and Community Is Changing the World* (2nd edition). Boise: Elevate, 2016.

Jobs, Steve. "You've Got to Find What You Love." Transcript of Speech Delivered at Stanford University, June 12, 2005. https://news.stanford.edu/2005/06/12/youve-got-find-love-jobs-says/

Jordan, Mary, and Kevin Sullivan. "The New Reality of Old Age in America." *The Washington Post.* September 30, 2017. www.washingtonpost.com/graphics/2017/national/seniors-financial-insecurity/

Kangas, Olli, Signe Jauhiainen, Miska Simaneinen, and Minna Ylikanno. *Experimenting with Unconditional Basic Income: Lessons from the Finnish BI Experiment 2017–2018.* Cheltenham: Edward Elgar, 2021.

Keynes, John Maynard. "Economic Possibilities for our Grandchildren." In *Essays in Persuasion,* 358–373. New York: WW. Norton & Company, 1963.

Lysova, Evgenia I., Jennifer Tosti-Kharas, Christopher Michaelson, Luke Fletcher, Catherine Bailey, and Peter McGhee. "Ethics and the Future of Meaningful Work: Introduction to the Special Issue." *Journal of Business Ethics* 185 (2023): 713–723. https://doi.org/10.1007/s10551-023-05345-9

McQuaid, Darius. "Gen Z and Millennial Workers More Tech Savvy Than Older Workers." *HR Review.* Accessed February 27, 2024. https://hrreview.co.uk/hr-news/gen-z-and-millennial-workers-more-tech-savvy-than-older-workers/124914

Organisation for Economic Cooperation and Development. "Hours Worked." Accessed February 27, 2024. https://data.oecd.org/emp/hours-worked.htm. https://doi.org/10.1787/47be1c78-en

Rawls, John. "The Priority of Right and Ideas of the Good." *Philosophy & Public Affairs* 17, no. 4 (1988): 251–276.

Rothstein, Jed (Director). *WeWork: Or the Making and Breaking of a $47 Billion Unicorn.* Hulu, 2021. Documentary film.

Schor, Juliet B. *The Overworked American: The Unexpected Decline of Leisure.* New York: Basic Books, 1993.

Schwab, Klaus. *The Fourth Industrial Revolution.* New York: Crown Business, 2016.

Taylor, Chris. "Three Reasons Universal Basic Income Pilots Haven't Led to Policy Change – Despite Their Success." *The Conversation*. April 11, 2022. Accessed February 27, 2024. https://theconversation.com/three-reasons-universal-basic-income-pilots-havent-led-to-policy-change-despite-their-success-180062

Van Parijs, Philippe. "Why Surfers Should Be Fed: The Liberal Case for an Unconditional Basic Income." *Philosophy & Public Affairs* 20, no. 2 (1991): 101–131.

World Economic Forum. "The Future of Jobs Report 2023." Accessed February 27, 2024. www.weforum.org/publications/the-future-of-jobs-report-2023/in-full/

World Economic Forum. "Global Risks 2024." Accessed February 27, 2024. www.weforum.org/publications/global-risks-report-2024/

Index

Note: Page numbers in **bold** indicate a table on the corresponding page.

For Product Safety Concerns and Information please contact our EU
representative GPSR@taylorandfrancis.com
Taylor & Francis Verlag GmbH, Kaufingerstraße 24, 80331 München, Germany

www.ingramcontent.com/pod-product-compliance
Ingram Content Group UK Ltd.
Pitfield, Milton Keynes, MK11 3LW, UK
UKHW021027180425
457613UK00021B/1096